Living the Awakened Heart

Lama Shenpen Hookham

First edition: April 2003

This edition: June 2015

Published for the Awakened Heart Sangha by:

The Shrimala Trust
Hermitage of the Awakened Heart
Ynys Grainog, Criccieth
Gwynedd, LL52 0NT
Email: office@ahs.org.uk

The Shrimala Trust is a registered charity (no. 1078783) and
limited company (no. 3880647) that supports the activity of
the Awakened Heart Sangha. The Awakened Heart Sangha is
a spiritual community formed by students of Lama Shenpen
Hookham.

Contents

Introduction

This booklet is about long-term training in the Awakened Heart Sangha. It is written for students who are making, or thinking of making, the Awakened Heart Sangha their spiritual home, the spiritual community they are supported by and support in return. It gives an idea of what it means to be training in the Awakened Heart Sangha.

Living the Awakened Heart is intended to be read alongside its companion book, *A Lifetime of Practice*. While this book gives you an overview of the content and context of the teachings, *A Lifetime of Practice* describes the structure of the Awakened Heart Sangha, and gives an overview of how the student progresses through the training.

I call the training that we are all involved in for the rest of our lives, 'Living the Awakened Heart'. It is a way of living and a way of dying, a vision and a path to Awakening for ourselves and all beings. It is a matter of really living what we are learning about the Awakened Heart, so that it does truly Awaken in us. Our aim is, of course, to reach complete and perfect Awakening in this very life-time. However, even if we do not make it to complete and perfect Awakening, we can practise in such a way that we never lose our way, either in this life or future lives, and we actually support and inspire each other. At the very least, we can play our part, through the Awakened Heart

Sangha, in bringing the Dharma into the world for the benefit of everyone in this and in future generations.

Living the Awakened Heart is as much a preparation for death as it is for life. The whole training is about letting go of the attachments, anger, bitterness and confusion that can cause us such agony at the time of death. More than that, it is a daily training in how to rest in the Awakened Heart with confidence, the only way to face death with confidence and, of course, death may come any day. When we first set out on the path to Awakening, we may simply be looking for a better way to live our life, more open, clear and sensitive in our daily life situations. However, as our understanding deepens we start to realise that awareness is not something that comes and goes like the various things that appear to it. It is, in itself, beyond concepts of time and space. Concepts of time and space simply appear within it. This deeper understanding opens up new possibilities about what life and death really mean. This deepening awareness of significance and meaning is what enables us, eventually, to face death with confidence and to help others do the same.

The teachings and practice introduced in the 'Introduction to Formless Meditation', 'Discovering the Heart of Buddhism' and 'Trusting the Heart of Buddhism' courses are the foundations for the 'Living the Awakened Heart' training. They introduce you to the Awakened Heart and to how you might come to trust it and eventually awaken to it fully. Once you have this foundation, it is not time to move on to some other subject; there is no greater subject. Rather, it is time to just get on with living it: to begin the long journey, to undertake the great quest for Awakening.

'Living the Awakened Heart' is about walking this path together with our friends and mentors in the Sangha. It is about gradually aligning every part of our lives with the Awakened Heart, until we find that its power carries us along effortlessly in the direction of Awakening, like a river flowing down to the sea.

The Heart and Goal of the Training is Resting in the Awakened Heart

The Awakened Heart is our natural state of being. So the only practice is to rest in that or, since we find that so hard to do, to move towards resting in that. That is what our Formless meditation and daily life awareness practice is all about. This resting in our natural state, the Awakened Heart, is all we need to long for, the only aim we need to have in mind. By longing for this and trying to align ourselves with this, we help it to unfold within us.

What we call Formless meditation is what we all do in the Awakened Heart Sangha as our core practice. Whether a beginner or an experienced practitioner, the Formless meditation is both the foundation and cutting edge of our practice. What we are doing is trying to link into the practice of resting in the Awakened Heart as best as we can. For a long time it's a matter of occasionally getting tantalising hints or glimmers of something inspiring. For an advanced practitioner, for a really great yogin, it would mean resting in one's deep realisation of what the Awakened Heart is and what resting in it means. As we progress along the path it's somewhere between the two: more or less glimpses and resting, depending on the day! Nevertheless, whether or not we can truly rest or even glimpse, the practice works at a very deep level. We may feel we are not progressing in terms of how often we can glimpse or how long we can rest - yet, somehow, the very commitment to practice in this way is having a profound effect on our whole outlook and approach to life. This is the most important sign that the practice is working. It works at a very deep level, steadily hacking away almost imperceptibly at the very root of our delusion.

When we understand that the Awakened Heart is truly both the path and the goal, we do not hanker after all sorts of different practices. We understand that any practice we may engage in has one purpose only, which is to link into the Awakened Heart. It is by understanding this to be the purpose of all the different practices, that we are able to engage in any of them in the right way. If we do not understand this, there is a danger that we will grasp onto various practices in the wrong way and with the wrong expectations. This is how they can end up as merely distracting us from the real point of Dharma practice. We could end up with a whole collection of seemingly unrelated practices and a constant sense of feeling we are not doing any of them properly. So it is important to keep remembering that the point of all the different practices is to help us to rest in the Awakened Heart.

But if all practices are for this one essential point, resting in the naturalness of the Awakened Heart, why is it that it is so difficult to do? The problem is that we have lost our naturalness and simplicity. We lose it, moment by moment, by not recognising our essential nature. As soon as we do not recognise it, which is in a way a very simple mistake, we lose ourselves in world within world of complication. The complication obscures the simplicity of our natural state of being. We lose all sense of perspective; our vision is narrowed and begins to feel claustrophobic. We feel trapped and start looking for ways of escape. In this state it is very hard to simply let go and be simple. Even when we think that we have let go a little or even a lot, our vision still seems to be narrow and restricted. On investigation, we find that there are all sorts of habits of mind, emotions and preconceived ideas that are still obstructing and hindering us, stopping us from recognising our true nature and from resting in it. All the different kinds of practices that there are in the Buddhist tradition are ways to help highlight these habits, emotions and preconceptions, drawing our attention to them and giving us the opportunity to let them go.

So you could say that the path to Awakening is about reversing what is fundamentally a very simple mistake. That mistake is to not recognise our own Awakened Heart that is present from the very beginning. How we miss it and turn away from it is a subtle and deep mystery, although fundamentally it is a single, simple mistake. The path is about recognising (gaining insight into) that mistake and letting go into the reality that is there when we do not make that mistake. That reality is experienced spontaneously as the joy and love of our natural responsiveness. All the complications that obstruct our recognition of this and all the suffering that these obstructions bring us emanate from that one fundamental mistake. If we can reverse that mistake, then the whole complicated structure built on it collapses by itself. So although we may do lots of practices to help us recognise and let go of layer upon layer of confusion and complication, there is always the possibility that we could simply rest in the Awakened Heart right here and now and all the confusion and complication would collapse by itself.

It is important to always bear this in mind, with a sense of gentle irony. All our efforts on the path are in a way unnecessary, since all we need to do, really, is reverse that one simple mistake and rest at ease in our true nature. It is only because we are so complicated that it seems we progress stage by stage, by letting go of obstructions bit by bit.

Knowing that the Awakened Heart is actually completely accessible at every moment can instil in us a strong sense of underlying confidence in our true nature and in the path. This kind of confidence is more important than any other quality we may gain from following the path. This is the confidence that keeps us on the path throughout life and death. It is the confidence to be open and simple, whatever the situation, and this protects us from confusion and complication.

As practitioners, we need to familiarise ourselves with all the different ways we find to ignore the real, the reliable, our true nature. We need to recognise how we, in fear, panic and confusion, try to grasp at what is not real, what is unreliable and deceptive. We need to gradually trace that grasping back to its origin, that simple mistake, avidya, the not recognising of our own true nature. That is how we learn to let go of increasingly subtle levels of grasping and confusion. Eventually, we can just rest in our uncontrived experience, the naturalness of the Awakened Heart, learning not to wander off down this slippery slope of grasping. It is like learning to walk a tightrope: we get on, we fall off, but we get back on again. We learn to balance, to rest in that space, letting reality be as it truly is.

This is what great yogins do. They rest in their true nature without falling into delusion. This is what it is all about. Everything we do in the Awakened Heart Sangha is directed at deepening and stabilising this practice, and we do this most simply and directly by not actually 'doing' anything. There is nothing to *do*, in the very deep sense of not trying to get rid of anything and not trying to attain anything. Into this space of non-doing arises spontaneous compassionate activity for the benefit of others. Resting in the Awakened Heart is the ultimate practice that is the essence of the path to Awakening. All Buddhist practices are ultimately intended to lead to this, and from it flow all the qualities and creative power of Awakened beings.

That is why, in this booklet I am giving the name 'resting in the Awakened Heart' to this ultimate goal of our practice. On the path, before we can rest in it truly or completely, we simply do our best to align with the Awakened Heart. Maybe we simply have a quiet confidence in the presence of the Awakened Heart as we sit in Formless meditation or go about our life. Maybe we simply touch on something genuine and real in our experience from time to time, possibly only for a fraction of a second at a time. This is what resting in the Awakened Heart is for us, until we reverse the mistake and enter that state of seeing the truth completely all the time.

I call this resting in the Awakened Heart the 'ultimate practice', to emphasise that it is not something we ordinarily do. To really rest like this is inconceivable, utterly beyond the reaches of our deluded minds. As practitioners, we cannot actually say 'Oh yes, my practice is just resting in my true nature'. Even the best of yogins, as long as they are still not completely awakened, are still very tentative in how they describe their practice. It would be tantamount to claiming to be enlightened to say that one was truly resting in this way.

However, right from the start of the path we have some inner feeling for what it might mean in our experience. This is because it is our nature and at some level we always know it. That is why we talk of discovering it within our experience and learning to trust it. It is already there in us as something to trust. It is as if we have the scent of it, a hint or the flavour of it, and we are sniffing through our experience trying to trace our way back to the source of that scent. Everything that is liberating and wholesome comes from aligning with the Awakened Heart and has the flavour of it. That is why we talk about our practice as learning to rest in the Awakened Heart. We are drawn by this hint or flavour and are trying to really taste it. In the end, though, we cannot taste it by trying and effort. In the end, *it* comes to us. In the end, we *give up* our contrived efforts and it is *then* that resting can start to happen. At first, we need effort and confidence. In the end, we only need relaxation and confidence. The same is true when we come to die. Confidence and relaxation are the only way.

Until we reach that kind of certainty, we seek and seek, nibbling at the boundaries of our understanding, trying to find the elusive source of the scent. But we cannot find it by 'trying', in the ordinary sense, because it is utterly outside of our deluded reference points of self and other, subject and object, time and space and so on. Instead, we hover on the edge of it, and then something magical happens. If we are open, something happens from outside our reference points and deluded efforts, we let go of our wrong view of things and are born into a new world, the Awakened World of the Awakened Heart. This might only last for a brief moment, but it is enough to give us the confidence that it is there, accessible, nearby and strangely familiar.

Although the most direct way of linking into the Awakened Heart is the Formless meditation and the daily life awareness practice associated with it, this is not at all to say that when we practise Formless meditation we are necessarily able to rest in the Awakened Heart. If only! Rather, it is our best approximation to it. When we sit in Formless meditation we are trying to link into the Awakened Heart as directly as we can. Here we are not using any particular form or method, but we are just trying to be it, right here and now; we are giving our best shot at being Awakened. This is not just fanciful imagination, because we do have some pointers and a flavour of what it is. We have verbal instructions (upadesha) and words we have found for ourselves that help us link into it, such as openness, letting be, and clarity. Furthermore, the Awakened Heart is actually right here within us, waiting to burst forth at any moment, if only we would let it.

What I am calling resting in the Awakened Heart or the ultimate practice is what is referred to by the terms Dzogchen and Mahamudra in the Tibetan tradition. Nowadays, people often say they like to practise Mahamudra or Dzogchen, but what they mean is that they are doing a practice like Formless meditation in which they try to link into the reality of Dzogchen or Mahamudra. It is worth making this point because, when we come to relate to the tradition, we do not want to be saying we are actually practising Dzogchen or Mahamudra, even though we are following that tradition. We can say instead that we are resting *(nyam shag)* in the Awakened Heart as best we can. At some point we hope to truly recognise the Awakened Heart as our true nature and be able to rest in it completely. This would be to realise Dzogchen or Mahamudra. It is the same as Awakening or Enlightenment.

First Things First

Having said all this, it is important to understand that, if we let our negative emotions run away with us, then not only are we not resting in the Awakened Heart but we are moving away from such a goal at a rapid rate. We are moving in the reverse direction to Awakening and trapping ourselves in a vicious circle of suffering and regret.

To notice our negative emotions arising from attachment, aversion and delusion, to turn towards them, let them be and let them go is what constitutes the first and most important part of our daily life awareness practice and is the foundation for any kind of Formless meditation practice. As we learn to be open to these emotions rather than being driven by them, our heart softens and our attitude, words and actions become gentler and more appropriate. This is what Trungpa Rinpoche called 'learning not to be a nuisance to the world'.

Strong emotions like anger and sexual desire are sometimes so overwhelming that simply working constantly, in order not to be totally overwhelmed by them, is sufficient in itself as our practice. In this situation we may feel that we are doing so badly that we are hardly practising Dharma at all; resting in the Awakened Heart seems merely a pipe dream.

There is no need to feel discouraged if you find this is the case. Simply to keep these strong emotions in check is in itself the path to Awakening, it *is* Dharma practice and we should not underestimate the accomplishment of learning to be able to do this. Even very advanced practitioners sometimes have to make dealing with strong emotions their main practice for a while. So learning to check them, even if we do not seem to achieve much else in life, is to have lived a life dedicated to Dharma. If the emotion you have to handle is very strong, then overcoming it again and again requires vigilance and steadfastness to remain open, clear and sensitive in the face of it. It is a powerful means of activating and empowering your Openness, Clarity, Sensitivity and linking into these qualities very strongly. Your very desperation helps with this. Think what a feeling of accomplishment you would have if you stopped someone committing a crime against humanity. The same feeling of accomplishment applies to learning to control your temper or your misplaced passions. So having strong emotions does not mean you are hopeless – those very emotions are actually a great Dharma stimulus and opportunity, if you have the courage and true-heartedness to rise to the challenge.

The Necessity and Pitfalls of Adopting a Variety of Practices

Even though I have been introduced to a variety of practices over my 35 years of training within the Kagyu and Nyingma traditions of Tibetan Buddhism, I find myself wanting to teach, above all else, my best understanding of the essential point, how to rest in the Awakened Heart. In this way, I hope to help genuine practitioners find their way around the plethora of imagery and ritual that seem sometimes to obscure, rather than reveal, the simplicity of Awakening that lies at their heart. In this I am following the example and heart advice of my own teachers.

Ultimately to rest in our true nature, the Awakened Heart, is the completion and perfection of all Dharma practices and all Dharma practices, whether one or many, are for attaining or accomplishing this ultimate practice. It is the one truth pointed to by all genuine spiritual traditions, Buddhist or otherwise. They are all pointing to the same thing, even though they may approach it from different angles or points of view.

It is because of the tangled web of obstacles and hindrances, which prevent us resting in the Awakened Heart, that so many and so varied Buddhist teachings and practices have arisen over the centuries for overcoming them. In the ultimate practice of resting in the Awakened Heart, there is no particular form to focus our attention on. It is called Formless practice, as opposed to other kinds of practice that involve focusing the attention on some kind of form, such as ideas or words. Nonetheless, the purpose behind using form is still the same as in formless practice. Such methods are simply using a less direct way of linking into the Awakened Heart. It is as if we use our imagination or words as a bridge into the ungraspable nature of reality. Even when we use words of upadesha such as to 'let go' or 'let be', we are using form in a subtle way. In some practices we use form more strongly, in order to become more aware of the nature of awareness, before letting the form go and resting again in formlessness, the ungraspable, open quality of the Awakened Heart.

The variety of possible forms is limitless, and the Buddhist tradition has evolved a vast number over the millennia. In the Awakened Heart Sangha we regularly use a number of forms, such as when we create a mandala of sacred space at our events, focus our practice at special times, make resolves and wishes concerning our practice, and give importance to our connections with the world of Awakening and other beings. All of these involve focusing on form in order to link into the Awakened Heart. Without focusing on these forms it would be very hard to simply rest in the Awakened Heart. We need more than the Formless meditation in order to keep on track, even though the Formless meditation is our most direct approximation to the ultimate practice

A point that has been recognised again and again by Tibetan yogins down the ages is that too many different practices can distract and overload the practitioner. In fact the Tibetans have a saying: 'The Indians took on and accomplished one practice and in so doing accomplished them all; the Tibetans take on many practices and in so doing accomplish none.' It would be too harsh to think this means that Tibetans do not accomplish anything through their many practices. It is simply a warning that this can easily happen. It is like a rich banquet from which each guest needs to select but a few dishes to satisfy himself or herself. It is only the chefs who need to know how to produce and preserve the recipes for them all.

Multiple practices can be particularly problematic in a group situation. There is a natural tendency to regard anything new, anything that is not given so much to beginners, as being more advanced. Our bored minds like the sound of new things, a new practice being like a new toy for us to play with. This is an example of what Trungpa Rinpoche spoke of as 'spiritual materialism'. To counter this he emphasised the importance of what he called 'cool boredom'. It is not really boredom in the ordinary sense, but is the dawning of the Openness that we are trying to avoid experiencing when we fidget about restlessly looking for entertainment all the time. It looks like death to the grasping mind, but when we really turn towards it whole-heartedly, we find that it is actually the spaciousness of our awareness, the true nature of our being. Trying to turn away from and escape this is what the Buddha meant by delusion and suffering! But it is something our minds easily fall into. This kind of tendency becomes even more difficult to avoid in a group situation. The tendency towards competitiveness exacerbates the situation: the idea that we are doing something 'advanced' is pleasing to our pride, making it seem that we are a higher class of person than the mere beginners. Similarly, we hate the idea of falling 'behind' our peers. So there are many pitfalls to be avoided when introducing more than one practice into a community of practitioners.

However, there is a real need to introduce other practices, because for almost everyone, at some point, they are necessary to deepen our practice. As we walk the path and draw closer to the ultimate practice, we discover that there are aspects to what is unfolding within us that we might never have thought of when first we heard about this way of working with our direct experience.

For example, at some point we will find that when confronted with other beings, our awareness manifests as a spontaneous love and desire to awaken them. In other words, we did not have to adopt a special practice in order to develop love and compassion. It simply arose spontaneously as we let go of grasping and attachment. Nevertheless, experience within the Buddhist tradition has shown that, by adopting practices that focus on love and compassion, this process is often speeded up. These practices are still powered by the same Openness, Clarity and Sensitivity that is the essence of our Formless meditation. But by focusing on love and compassion they highlight blocks or distortions in our openness and awareness and help us to let go of them. Focusing on love and compassion helps us work through the subtle obscurations that may be present in our imperfect Formless meditation, and may be preventing the inexpressibly vast love of our Awakened Heart from welling up within us.

Again, as we let go of more obvious, gross forms of grasping, we discover that we have, hidden in the background of our awareness, strange, distorted or unrealistic feelings or beliefs about how the world is.

For example, we discover an emotional attachment to ourselves and the things in our life as being somehow permanent and given. When we examine such feelings and beliefs, we find they are false and deluded. This inspires us to let them go. As we do this, we find that the way we contemplate the nature of reality in our meditation has deepened. Eventually, our awareness opens up into a wondrous vision of worlds and beings that interpenetrate beyond space and time, completely changing our view of what we and our world really are. Even though the simple practice of resting in the Awakened Heart would eventually, of itself, open out into this vaster vision, it has been found within the Buddhist tradition that this process can be speeded up by practices specifically designed to have that effect. It might involve reading life stories of Buddhist practitioners or sutra accounts of what the Buddha taught or did. It might involve rituals that reflect a whole different attitude to the nature of the cosmos and so on. These practices are still powered by the same Openness, Clarity and Sensitivity that is the essence of our Formless meditation. By focusing on vast and amazing ideas about how reality might really be, these practices highlight blocks or distortions in our openness and awareness and help us to let go of them. Exploring these ideas helps us notice and relax the grasping force in our awareness, which holds rigidly to an arbitrary and limited vision, that may be present, unnoticed, in our imperfect Formless meditation.

So, on the one hand, these changes in our experience and view of the world, such as the emerging compassion or expanding vision, are not actually the result of anything we do. It is simply that opening out in the direction of the ultimate practice involves us in a natural process in which this kind of thing happens by itself. These changes all ultimately flow out of our Formless meditation and awareness practice. On the other hand, if this is not what is happening in our practice, it is a sign that our meditation and awareness practice is veiled or obstructed. It is not quite accurate in some way, and so there might be other practices that could help us focus on and dissipate these obstructions to our Formless meditation.

We need to explore for ourselves the grasping habits that are obstructing our meditation, blocking our compassion and vision and so on. Such exploration might reveal deeply-entrenched negative attitudes towards ourselves and others or a rigidly held view of the Universe that rejects all sorts of possibilities.

In order to overcome these obstructions, there are different activities within the Buddhist tradition for drawing our attention to them. In fact, this is what all the myriad of practices the tradition has developed are for. Having had our attention drawn to the obstructions, we are in a position to choose to let them go. In this way, all the different activities and practices can be looked on as supports for Formless meditation and daily life awareness practice. They remove obstacles and blocks in it, helping us to let go in the direction of resting in the Awakened Heart, the ultimate practice. In theory, there is no need for a multitude of different practices, in practice, some of them could be of immense value and help.

Living the Awakened Heart & Traditional Tibetan Buddhism

At first glance, the 'Living the Awakened Heart' training may seem to have departed from the Tibetan tradition in terms of the colourful display that has come to be so strongly associated with Tibetan Buddhism. However, the training is actually entirely true to the essential heart of the tradition. Over the centuries, the Tibetan tradition of Buddhism has evolved and been shaped by the conditions and cultural preferences of the Tibetan people. Many compromises and adaptations were made in order to satisfy political rulers and powerful patrons. This was often seen to be the best way of preserving the teachings for sincere practitioners in future generations. Because Tibetan Buddhism was practised by the whole population of the country, it had to be accessible to people with a whole range of different spiritual aptitudes. So the emphasis was put on those practices that proved popular and suited the cultural mentality. Often this meant over-emphasising rites and rituals that had wide public appeal, rather than subtle teachings about the true meaning of these practices or how to rest in the true nature of our being. It would be wrong to conclude that the subtle teachings were, or are, neglected and not valued. It simply means that, if you want them, you have to know what you are looking for and ask for them. If you simply go along with what is happening publicly, you could easily get a lifetime of rites and rituals and not much connection with the inner meaning.

So in Tibetan Buddhism, certain customs and ways of teaching that are not essential have developed in response to social and historical situations. They might sometimes even be harmful for serious practitioners. For example, Tibetan Buddhism often appears to be about a seemingly endless variety of strange practices, such as visualizations, complicated rituals and numerous abhishekas (empowerments). These make it seem like a veritable obstacle course of hurdles and hoops that have to be jumped through as a necessary preliminary to receiving the highest teachings (the only ones that sound really meaningful or interesting to many of us). However, Tibetan Buddhism is more truly described as a vehicle for the live transmission of Awakening. The transmission is from yogins (practitioners with experience and realisation) to students, through skilful meditation instruction, helped and supported by various practices that vary from person to person, according to the needs and inclinations of both teachers and students. The skilful meditation instructions are referred to by various names, one of which in Sanskrit is upadesha (*mengak* in Tibetan).

My training was essentially that of a *mengakpa*, that is to say someone who receives oral meditation instruction (upadesha, *mengak*) from one or more experienced yogins. That instruction introduces one to the essential point, the Awakened Heart and how to rest in it. The student takes this point as the essence of the path and then pursues that path single-mindedly for the rest of his or her life, as realisation gradually dawns, deepens and stabilises. This one essential Formless practice usually needs to be supported by various other activities and practices to deepen a student's understanding and realisation of it. These practices do this by removing misunderstandings and obstructions, broadening one's vision, increasing one's confidence and revealing new aspects of the practice, which one might otherwise have missed.

The 'Living the Awakened Heart' training follows the model of the yogins of Tibet, those practitioners who really dedicated themselves to Awakening and worked with their direct experience in meditation to accomplish it. So it is true to the real heart of the tradition, although it may look a little different on the surface. I have checked with Khenpo Tsultrim Gyamtso Rinpoche to make sure that what I am giving my students is actually a complete training within the Dzogchen and Mahamudra tradition and he has confirmed that it is. There is nothing essential left out of the training, so you do not need to worry that, by following this training, you are missing out on some essential element. There are various teachings and practices that I may introduce as optional extras from time to time, but the core teachings and practices outlined in this booklet include all that is essential.

The Areas of the Training

In order to give you a clearer idea about what the 'Living the Awakened Heart' training involves, I have divided it into different areas, listed below. Although these areas are central to all Buddhist traditions, this particular group is not gathered into a formal list anywhere that I know of.

The areas of training are all ways of helping us align with the Awakened Heart in order to increase the effectiveness of our practice of resting in the Awakened Heart. If we were resting in the Awakened Heart in the right way, love and compassion for all beings would well up, clarity of understanding of ungrasped reality would shine forth, our actions in relation to the world would be spontaneously apt and skilful for the benefit of others, our vision of the world would expand to see far beyond our present limited horizons, our ability to fulfil all our wishes would be spontaneously accomplished and we would be filled with the inspiration and adhistana of the world of Awakening. Since this is not happening, or only happening to a limited extent, we need to train in the six corresponding areas to help remove obstacles and align ourselves better with the Heart of Awakening.

I introduce all these areas in 'Discovering the Heart of Buddhism' and 'Trusting the Heart of Buddhism' and then elaborate on them in my teachings at courses and retreats. Every area has aspects that we can connect to in our experience, as well as aspects that touch on traditional Buddhist doctrines the truth of which we cannot yet see in our experience. All areas are common to both 'Discovering the Heart of Buddhism' and 'Trusting the Heart of Buddhism', and I teach them all at both Heart of Awakening events and Vaster Vision events. All these areas are fundamental, and can be understood on many different levels. I intend to do more intensive courses in all these areas and build up teaching materials, based on those courses, for students who were not present. Furthermore, one should not make too much of the somewhat arbitrary distinctions between these areas. All the areas are taught for the sole purpose of helping us to link into the Awakened Heart, so what is important is this that they have in common, not their differences.

The areas of training are:

- **Love and Compassion** – The practice common to all great spiritual traditions that underpins the whole Path to Awakening.

- **Insight Into Emptiness or Nature of Mind** – this practice is distinctively Buddhist. It cuts through confusion and is the immediate cause of Awakening and thus liberation from samsara. In Tibetan Buddhism this includes pointing out instructions.

- **Daily Life Awareness and Mindfulness Practice** – applying practice within our daily life. This area of practice is about mindfulness of body, speech and mind and how to use whatever situation you are in as Dharma practice. It is about generosity, discipline and patience and so on. It covers a range of areas such as body awareness, truthful and sensitive communication, the precepts, Dharma art and so on. All these practices relate to a deeper understanding of our personal mandala of body, speech, mind/heart and environment. They make immediate sense in terms of leading a happy life and are not necessarily in themselves Buddhist or conducive to the goal of liberation from samsara. In the Awakened Heart Sangha we seek to extend them by linking them to the other areas of *Living the Awakened Heart* so that they are conducive to Liberation.

- **There is More to Dying than Death** - At whatever stage in your practice you are, you are advised to read the book entitled 'There is More to Dying than Death'. This gives you the basic orientation and information you need for facing life and death and incorporating the awareness of the inevitability of death into the whole of your path. You are advised to return to it often and at least on an annual basis. Around the time of celebrating the Buddha's Enlightenment and the consecration of the Stupa at the Hermitage, the Sangha holds a day on which we reflect on death, those who have died and how to prepare for our own death.

In order to make sense of taking Refuge in the Buddha, Dharma and Sangha, we have to understand the depth and scope of the Buddhist worldview. We need to understand how it describes the Path to Awakening and how to engage in it. The following three areas of training deepen our understanding of that worldview and the path, including the meaning of the Three Refuges and how they are able to protect and guide us in this life and beyond.

- **Vaster Vision of the Buddhist Worldview** – studying and reflecting on the teachings in Buddhist sutras and commentaries that describe and explain the stages of the Path of Awakening and Liberation, including karma, and how ignorance and clinging tie us to endless rebirths in samsara.

- **Making Pranidhanas** (vows, resolves, aspirations or wishing prayers) – the practice that focuses, strengthens and drives all our practice day and night and includes honing our motivation and vision, taking vows such as Refuge and Bodhisattva Vows, making prayers and aspirations, reciting liturgy and so on.

- **Making Connections** in Order to Intensify Punya (the power of goodness) and adhishtana (blessing power) – this is about applying Mandala Principle in relation to the Mandala of Awakening. All Buddhist ritual and customs relate to this. It includes relating to teachers and realised beings, sacred objects, substances, sounds and places, life-stories and so on, through making offerings, prostrations or circumambulations etc.

Love and Compassion

As has already been mentioned, since Openness, Clarity and Sensitivity are the essence of true love and compassion, simply to move towards resting in the Awakened Heart in one's Formless Meditation is in itself to be training in spontaneous and equal love and compassion for all beings. However, because of our non-recognition of our true nature, we are trapped in grasping habits of fear, attachment and narrowness of vision. These are the deeply entrenched habits of the ego-mandala with all the strategies it displays to protect and pamper itself. Often these go unnoticed in our formless practice and it is not until situations provoke a reaction that we even notice these habits are there.

There are, therefore, practices in Buddhism that use an element of form or imagination in order to draw these grasping habits to our attention by actually stirring them up. This shows us what we need to let go of. The way to let go is as is described in the Formless meditation. It always comes back to the same thing. For example, there is a practice called the Apramanas (limitless love, compassion, joy and equanimity) which throws into sharp relief our difficulty with wishing well to ourselves or to those we would rather not have anything to do with. By imagining feeling love for ourselves and all beings equally, we notice where our grasping habits are and we can gradually train ourselves to let them go and rest in the naturalness of limitless and equal love for all beings.

Apramanas

Apramana means measureless and the Apramanas practice refers to a structured way of reflecting and meditating that links us into the measureless love, compassion, sympathetic joy and equanimity that resides naturally, but hidden' in our hearts' In general, I suggest people start thinking about practising the Apramanas after they have been practising Formless meditation for at least one or two years and are starting to settle into a regular practice of about an hour a day' I think it is important for people to have some experience in practising the Apramanas before taking the Bodhisattva vow'

Tonglen

Tonglen (sending and taking) is a practice that can be introduced and practised on many different levels. It means literally to send out goodness to others and take their suffering on yourself. In general, the foundation for this important practice is laid by several years of formless meditation and Apramanas practice. However, there is a way of practising it even before doing the Formless practice, almost as a means of settling into it. I am starting to teach Tonglen in this way now, because people have found it in books and have told me how helpful they have found it, even when they could not settle to meditation. I thought about this a lot for several years before deciding to start introducing this preliminary practice of Tonglen as an experiment. It is a very helpful practice when you are feeling very negative, or suffering a lot, or having to work with others who are suffering a lot.

Activities that support our training in love and compassion are:

Reviewing again and again reflections in 'Discovering the Heart of Buddhism' and 'Trusting the Heart of Buddhism' that help us open our hearts to others

Meditation on the Apramanas, Tonglen (Sending out good to others and taking their suffering onto ourselves) and Lojong (training or purifying the heart)

Insight Into Emptiness or Nature of Mind

Ultimately, resting in our own true nature, the Awakened Heart, is to penetrate its depths, to see it in its fullness, clearly, without obstruction. However, this seeing does not come naturally. We are too hide-bound by our assumptions about the nature of the Universe and of our experience. We take it as given, for example, that the mind is inside the head without noticing that the inside of our head is an idea or thought that arises in the mind – this fact is extremely mysterious! Asking ourselves questions such as 'where is the mind?' helps us to focus on the true nature of experience. We have to ask ourselves such seemingly naive questions, in order to start to focus on the assumptions that veil our understanding and let them go. In this way the mysterious Openness of our being can gradually reveal itself.

The sense of understanding opening up, as we let go of grasping, occurs naturally as we engage in the practice of Formless meditation. However, without introducing this process of experiential questioning, this particular way of focusing on our experience, we could go for years or even life times without noticing the hidden assumptions that are distorting our understanding. The questioning makes the difference between the calming practice of shamatha (peaceful abiding, Tib. *shinay*) and the liberating practice of vipashyana (insight into truth, Tib. *hlagtong*).

The kind of questioning that I am referring to here is not intellectual analysis in the sense that we are trying to work out a theoretical answer that hangs together logically. It is more a matter of opening out to our experience with a sense of wonder at the strangeness of it. So it's a matter of openness and wonderment, not grasping. It focuses on experience and leaves us simply with the experience as it is, stripping away all our assumptions and the notions that we use to 'explain' it. This requires a special kind of precision, honesty and courage. More than anything, it requires the courage to face and accept what we do not know and that can be quite frightening and disorientating.

Generally speaking, the process of dismantling our assumptions does not happen all at once. We need to keep approaching our experience from new angles, asking different questions as we recognize different kinds of belief structure that we unconsciously grasp or hold in the background of our awareness and which obstruct our understanding. These are not necessarily beliefs that we can or do justify intellectually, or are even aware of. For example, we put so much energy into securing and protecting the self, although intellectually we are very uncertain as to what it is. Our emotions and actions bear witness to our passionate belief in it and in its existing in a particular way. By examining closely what we mean by 'self' and noticing the inconsistencies and confusion surrounding it, we can start to recognise our grasping at what is false and therefore needs to be let go of. This requires openness and clarity in the form of a powerful kind of honesty that takes a keen interest in what is real and true, just because it is true.

Having recognized our grasping at false beliefs and habits of thinking, effort and discipline is required in noticing them and letting them go. Sometimes grasping at a whole series of false beliefs and habits of thinking can collapse temporarily in one go and we can see right through to the essence or heart of Reality. Nevertheless, the old habits still need to be worn out like old boots. So practices that involve constantly questioning our assumptions and habitual ways of thinking are essential. The quality of interest and honesty required here is called prajna, which is sometimes translated as intelligence (or wisdom). It is not intelligence in the sense of being clever with words and concepts. It is intelligence in the sense of being honest and accurate in our appreciation of our own experience.

It is important to have a deep and strong sense of the adhistana (supportive influence or blessing) of Awakening to support us in this kind of practice. This is both because it is through the adhistana of Awakening that realization is possible and because sudden strong experiences (nyams) of emptiness or Reality can be frightening. They loom like death itself to the grasping ego mandala. This links to the sixth area of the training explored in this booklet, but needs to be mentioned here to alert the practitioner to its importance. The sense of adhistana that is needed provides us with a sense of letting go into something more real and alive than the delusions we are letting go of. This is what gives us the confidence to let go - it overcomes our fear.

Sometimes, when questioning, we can find ourselves pushing too hard to find intellectual answers. The remedy for this is to relax and have confidence that the answer will come through on its own, not through our intellectual grasping, but from the adhistana of Awakening itself. We may start to feel that we are not clever enough intellectually to understand such deep things, but this is not the point. We only need to be honest. Honesty is already extremely intelligent and the only intelligence we need. We don't need to be particularly clever or articulate. So whether we are very gifted academically or not, we all need the same kind of openness and honesty to be able to ask our questions in a naïve and simple way. We also need to be able to open to the adhistana of Awakening coming to us from beyond intellectual grasping.

What makes this kind of questioning a special area of training over and above the simple Formless meditation is that it requires, at least at first, a certain amount of form. By 'form' I mean something to focus on. Whereas in the formless practice proper there is nothing to focus on, there is simply resting in the nature of awareness itself, in this kind of questioning we use a question to focus our attention. We use the form of the question to draw our attention to hidden assumptions. The form that is introduced to start with may be quite gross, such as repeating the question again and again to ourselves, but it draws our attention to aspects of our experience we might otherwise have missed. Having had our attention drawn to our experience in this way, the habitual patterns of thought that were obstructing our vision drop away, maybe just for a fraction of a second. We are then able to experience our experience very simply, as it is, for a moment, before the old habits kick in again. It's as if, having had such an experience, we can return to it almost like revisiting a place. By returning to that place again and again, our old way of thinking gradually starts to wear thin, allowing us to rest more easily and naturally in greater clarity. As this happens, the question becomes less and less necessary. What is happening is that we are moving closer to resting in the Awakened Heart, the whole purpose of the formless practice. Eventually we can drop the focus provided by the questioning entirely, because the intelligence that is the true nature of the questioning is none other than the Openness, Clarity and Sensitivity of our Awakened Heart.

Activities that support our investigation into our experience are:

Questions about our experience introduced in 'Discovering the Heart of Buddhism' and 'Trusting the Heart of Buddhism', especially in regard to spaciousness of awareness and not-self

'Analytical' meditations like those in *Progressive Stages of Meditation on Emptiness*

Specific preliminary meditations from the Dzogchen and Mahamudra traditions

Study, reflection and meditation on the instructions contained in texts such as *Clarifying the Natural State* by Dagpo Tashi Namgyal, and the *Mahamudra Pranidhana* of Karmapa Rangjung Dorje.

Daily Life Awareness and Mindfulness Practice

Resting in the Awakened Heart, our own true nature, the nature of the Universe, leads naturally to being able to act spontaneously and appropriately for the benefit of others. When we can rest in this way, there is no need to keep to special rules or codes of behaviour. This is the special yogin's conduct beyond giving up negative acts and adopting positive ones. Although this is a very advanced level of practice, we begin to notice this happening to some extent almost as soon as we start out on the path to Awakening. As we open towards our experience in meditation and daily life awareness practice with courage and honesty, we already find we respond to situations more sensitively, with more kindness and more appropriately. Since Openness, Clarity and Sensitivity are our nature, the more we let go of our distorted habits of thinking and behaving, the more our behaviour is in line with our natural responsiveness and sense of wellbeing. We naturally become more gentle, communicative and clear in our dealings with others and with the world in general.

However, it would be mistaken to think that this means that we should concentrate exclusively on our Formless meditation and not worry about our conduct; sloppily disregarding the effects of our actions, smugly secure in our idea of ourselves as Dharma people whose conduct will naturally be all right. Just as with all the other areas of the training, examining our relationship with the world can reveal to us negative attitudes that we might not notice when sitting in Formless meditation. Yet such attitudes will be blocking the process of opening into the Openness, Clarity and Sensitivity of our true nature. Although, in theory, appropriate action arises spontaneously from resting in our true nature - in practice, our inappropriate attitudes, reflected in our speech and actions, prevent us resting in this way. So noticing and letting go of negative actions, speech and reactions (in our general behaviour in relation to the world) is integral to our daily life awareness practice and fundamental in terms of making progress with the Formless meditation. As we let go of negative attitudes, speech and actions, they are naturally replaced by their positive counterparts. As we notice this, we need to cultivate those positive tendencies and actions, since they are in harmony with the Openness, Clarity and Sensitivity of our true nature and are conducive to the awakening of these qualities in our Formless practice.

Inappropriate attitudes often express themselves in the way we relate to our own body, as well as to others and the world in general. So applying awareness practice to our own body can provide vital triggers of awareness, enabling us to let go of inappropriate attitudes and making it more obvious to us how to let go of the negative speech and actions that flow from them.

Our Physical Presence in the World

There is a feedback process between our awareness, how we act in the world, and how we experience our presence in the world. It is not by accident that a person who leads a good life is called 'upright', an untrustworthy person is called 'shifty' and a trustworthy person is called 'solid' and 'grounded'.

Becoming aware of our physical body links directly to the Formless practice. The Awakened Heart that we are learning to rest in includes our physical presence in the world. The physical body is experienced as the very awareness that we are learning to rest in. Since awareness of the body is an intrinsic aspect of awareness in general, the more we rest in the nature of awareness, the more relaxed, confident, open, clear and sensitive we will feel physically. It can be very helpful to deliberately focus on body awareness and perhaps use simple, gentle exercises as a means of linking into this awareness of the body. Furthermore, through feeling more alive and relaxed physically, our actions of body, speech and mind become more open, clear and sensitive to ourselves and others.

For example, if we feel tense and do not know how to relax physically, it is very difficult to be open, clear and sensitive in the way we communicate with others. Simply by becoming aware of the tension, acknowledging it and doing something physical to release it, we can be more open, clear and sensitive. This is a very simple and obvious example, but it reflects the deep and subtle nature of body awareness.

Life Style

One of the most important things we need to constantly review and reflect on is our life-style in general. Is it conducive to following the path to Awakening? How could it be made more so? It is important that this should come into consideration when making life decisions about career, family commitments, financial commitments and so on. If you really want to follow the path to Awakening whole-heartedly, think about what this means in terms of commitment. How many other things can you take on as well? Of course, if we are already committed to relationships and situations, we are going to have to work within the constraints laid down by them. There is no need to feel discouraged, as if it is not possible to make a whole range of different kinds of life-style a way of following the path to Awakening. However, this is not to underestimate how important it is to make sure the major decisions in our life are motivated first and foremost by our commitment to the path to Awakening. This means being clear about our values and priorities. This takes training. Often, it is because we are not clear at a deep and fundamental level, that we more or less 'let life live us', making us feel less free and more constrained than we are. This is where it is important to recognise harmful and time consuming attachments that are ultimately simply hindrances on the path to Awakening. We may decide that, for us, having a partner, job and family is the best way forward, but if we think we really need all these things before all else, we are just falling into samsara's trap. This shows up in our general attitude towards life and to others. It is as if we try to juggle a whole lot of different value systems at once and it's just by chance which one happens to land in our hand at the moment of making a life decision. We really need to train in order to be clear about the path to Awakening and what is really conducive to it and to put this first in every decision we take in life.

Attachment is a sign of lack of confidence in the path to Awakening. So simply reflecting on what is truly important in life can protect us at moments when we falter through lack of confidence. It is so easy to suppress our wish for Awakening at key moments, while we let ourselves be driven by our conditioned responses, attachments, hopes and fears. If we have taken care to make our life decisions in harmony with the path to Awakening, then we buy ourselves time, as it were, in which to overcome this lack of confidence. Once we have taken decisions that commit us to a life of attachment and worldly concerns, it is sometimes difficult to reverse it and our opportunity to overcome our lack of confidence in the path to Awakening seems to slip out of reach, sometimes for a very long time indeed.

A Relaxed and Playful Approach to Life

Whatever our life-style, relaxing, resting, simple walking meditation, playing and so on can provide important support to the Formless practice of just letting be, just resting in the Awakened Heart. It is important not to think that we stop practising when we rest. Rest and play are essential aspects of practice.

Whatever our life-style, on the path to Awakening, too much busy-ness is a sign of laziness and distraction. It is a sign that we have become caught up in grasping and attachment to this and that. It is wasting time. To be relaxed and playful, letting things be, not being fussy, not having lots of notions about what is right and wrong, good and bad, being content with whatever happens and so on are all signs of a good practitioner who knows how to act in the world. As long as you are not grasping you are not wasting time.

Setting Boundaries - Precepts

Until we are quite advanced yogins, we will find it very useful to have some boundary markers that act as triggers of awareness. When we cross these, they prompt us to stop and take a hard look at our behaviour, helping us not to stray too far out of line with our heart wish. Boundary markers may take the form of binding commitments such as formally taking precepts from a preceptor and undertaking not to do certain negative things or to do certain positive things. For retreatants there are various boundary markers in terms of retreat rules. Another form of boundary marker is the various checklists of negative and positive actions in the Buddha's teachings that we can use as reminders of what kind of behaviour we aspire to keep to.

For example, the five most basic precepts for any Buddhist are not to kill, steal, lie and behave irresponsibly sexually or with intoxicants. So when we are tempted to do any of these things, remembering these boundary markers sharpens our awareness and we think carefully about our conduct. With all of these precepts, I encourage people to relate to them as having two separate parts. On the one hand, as referring to extremely negative actions that we undertake not to do (for example, murder another human being), while on the other hand, as referring to negative actions that we need to try to avoid, while cultivating their positive counterparts (for example, to try not to kill any sentient life and to always try to save life).

The Buddhist tradition lays much store by precepts and has many lists and codes of behaviour. It is important not to miss the wood for the trees though. In general the precepts are a rather rough and ready way of protecting our practice, until we get to the point where spontaneous right conduct flows naturally from resting in the Awakened Heart. I do not find that there is a great need to emphasise very strongly the five basic precepts for people in our society, as most of us are basically law-abiding anyway. However, for those who come for Buddhist teachings who are murderers, liars, thieves, rapists or drunkards it is important to stress the five basic precepts before all else!

In the Awakened Heart Sangha, we use the precepts as part of our training to bring our behaviour in daily life in line with resting in the Awakened Heart. When we look into our hearts, we find our deepest heart wish and we find a kind of feeling for how we want to be in ourselves and how we want to be in relationship to others. This is what we link into by means of our meditation and daily life awareness practice. When we do this successfully, our thoughts, words and actions naturally emanate from that heart wish and are naturally open, clear and sensitive. However, for a long time, this is not quite what happens in practice. We find we are not often fully aligned to our heart's deepest wish and we often act in closed, unclear and insensitive ways.

That is why generally speaking, it is important to train in, and to adopt, practices that are specifically about how to relate to the world and others. We have to train in living our life in a way that causes the least harm to any being and the greatest benefit for as many as we can, in both the long and the short term.

In practice, it is not easy to totally avoid harming others and to truly benefit them in the short term and it is only the Dharma that helps in the long term. It is so often the case that in benefiting one person, we deprive or even harm others; or by trying to please everyone, we end up pleasing nobody; or by trying to do what we think is best, we inadvertently create as many problems as we solve, and so on. We have to live with the unsatisfactoriness of this and not lose heart. We can use such experience to deepen and strengthen our faith in the path to Awakening and to help us give up excessive busy-ness and feelings of over-responsibility. Actions with the genuine intention to help others have a self-existent goodness, irrespective of the practical outcome.

However, when we try to act in more positive ways, we often find we come up against all kinds of blocks and distortions. So the training is to notice these and learn to let them go, by means of the awareness practice that we learn in meditation. This alerts us to habitual mistakes and reactions that are hindering us and need to be overcome, such as attachment, meanness, laziness, pride, jealousy, paranoia, anger, hatred, irritation, discouragement and delusion. These scatter our energy and prevent us meditating and deepening our understanding.

Being honest and open, allowing ourselves to feel the unsatisfactoriness and the messiness of situations, not grasping at a false sense of being sure and right about what we do in every situation, are all training in openness. Responding from the heart and giving the situation our best shot is training in clarity and sensitivity. Once we have given it our best shot, we can let go into a sense of ease and confidence, allowing ourselves peace of mind. Working with our conduct like this is part of our Dharma training and flows from and also reinforces our Formless practice. We can use the precepts to help us; but we have to be careful to keep the right touch about them, using them as helpful triggers of awareness. This means, on the one hand, not being complacent about them, and on the other, not being obsessive or legalistic about them.

As time goes on and we understand the Buddhist world-view more deeply, we may find that we take a different attitude to the likely consequences of our actions. We tend to start off by thinking about the consequences of our actions on this life and on this world. However, the Buddhist world-view takes into account the consequences our actions have on future lives in ways we cannot know from our direct experience. This all comes into consideration in the section on understanding the nature of being.

At the end of 2001 and on into 2002, I wrote quite extensively on 'Buddhism Connect' about Buddhist precepts and rules of conduct. I recommend students to look at these emails and raise any issues arising from them with me. They are meant to give guidance when we are faced with difficult moral dilemmas in relation to the world and others.

Activities that support our training in how to act in and relate to the world and others:

Reviewing sections in 'Discovering the Heart of Buddhism' and 'Trusting the Heart of Buddhism' that relate to right intention and action, especially clarity, mandala principle and change of heart

Making sure that we carry our meditation and awareness practice into our daily life and noticing how it affects and helps others.

Developing awareness of our body

Reflection on and commitment to traditional Buddhist precepts and right conduct as found, for example, in *The Jewel Ornament of Liberation* by Gampopa, translated by Khenpo Konchog Gyaltsen Rinpoche, chapters.12-17.

There is More to Dying than Death

Although the best time to read and reflect on death is before we have to face it – preferably a long time beforehand – few people do so. It is symptomatic of the human condition that life's preoccupations sweep us relentlessly on, leaving us with no time to think about death, and little inclination to do so. This is one reason why the prospect of death tends to come as a shock, when we are suddenly faced, at the worst possible moment, with fundamental questions about what life is, or was, all about. At that time, more likely than not, we will be scared, unable to believe what is happening, worried about doing the right thing, worried about how to avoid pain, about doing the right thing, worried about how to avoid pain, worried about what we dare to hope for. Even when we have tried to prepare ourselves well in advance, death, by its very nature, still tends to come as a shock and can evoke emotions we scarcely knew were possible.

It is understandable that those who do not believe there is any reality deeper than this life, and the death that ends it, do not want to dwell on the fact of death. But if you suspect there is a way to awaken to a deeper timeless reality that lies beyond birth and death, there is nnothing more compelling than reflection upon death. Inspiration and joy can be found in doing so, since it turns one's thoughts away from attachment to what is unreal, and leads one in the direction of what is ultimately real and of lasting value. It is said to have lasting value because the true nature of our being that the Buddha discovered is one of genuine, unfailing joy, meaning, freedom, the cessation of suffering, and the endless power to relieve the sufferings of others, spontaneously and effortlessly.

I have written a book called *'There's More to Dying than Death: A Buddhist Perspective'* which I encourage all my students to read. You can purchase a copy online.

Vaster Vision of the Buddhist Worldview

The nature of the path is such that our vision opens up more and more as we move towards resting in the true nature of our being. We gain deeper insight into Openness, Clarity and Sensitivity, the mysterious nature of being that we share with everyone else, the heart of Reality itself. However, because of our veils and obstructions, we often do not see certain aspects of the truth, simply because we are not expecting to see them. We are expecting to see the world in the same old way and so we do. That is why there are so many teachings about the nature of reality beyond what we can now see for ourselves. These teachings are attempts by Awakened beings to describe what they have discovered about the nature of the universe and how they see it. We don't need to believe all these things. In fact, as the true nature of reality is inconceivable, it hinders our insight if we cling too heavily to any kind of notion about the way things are, even one derived from Buddhist teachings. However, simply hearing these things can unsettle our ordinary assumptions, allowing us to notice that they are indeed assumptions and that we could let go of them. Even by letting go of them a little, we can get a hint or an inkling of how reality might be and this might be enough to allow deeper insights to break through. So learning about and wondering about the descriptions of reality given by Awakened beings is actually a way of opening ourselves to a much deeper appreciation of what we might discover in our experience.

Knowing about the vaster vision revealed by Awakened beings is a way of deepening our motivation to penetrate to the very heart of reality. Without this vision we might be content with some lesser goal and never realize our full potential to help others. For example, we might think that we had achieved the goal simply by being somewhat more open, clear and sensitive than we had been previously. This would stop us seeking further and give us a false sense of security. But the vaster vision protects us from complacency, suggesting there might be more to Awakening than we thought, prompting us to look deeper. Another common problem that arises through not having the full vision of the nature of the path is that we become attached to our nyams (experiences in meditation). For example, if great bliss arises in our meditation, it is easy to want to simply maintain it for as long as possible. When we find we can't, we feel frustrated and hanker after a repeat of the experience, rather than genuinely seeking the path to Awakening. We might have the problem of setting our sights too low, believing that we do not have the power to liberate all beings. It is only by believing in our full potential that we can in fact actualise it. It is very easy to believe in some lesser goal that satisfies our ego mandala wishes, but has nothing to do with Awakening.

The vaster vision provides suggestions to us that we can explore. It prompts us to take seriously things in our experience that otherwise we might simply have dismissed. It's not that we need to take it all on board and 'sign on the dotted line'. Rather, by listening to the teachings coming down to us through the tradition, we are encouraged to explore possibilities and facets of our experience that our existing entrenched view of the world told us were unimportant. For example, if we do not know about the Buddha nature and that love and compassion are intrinsic to the nature of the universe, we might treat moments of love and compassion in our experience as mere sentimentality and attachment. The teaching that they are actually our true nature bursting through makes them more interesting and something to take seriously. By opening to those experiences, we can link into the nature of reality itself, in a way we would not have been able to do if we had dismissed them out of hand. Similarly, if we have never heard of the idea of adhistana, that reality is alive and has a power to Awaken us, we might always think it was all up to self effort. This would prevent us ever learning to really relax properly. By wondering about and reflecting on teachings about adhistana, we might get a hint or inkling of how it might be to relax more and trust in the process of Awakening to unfold within itself. In this way, we might discover in our own experience that this is the only way to really rest in the Awakened Heart.

As we become familiar with the vaster vision of the Buddhist tradition, it tends to soak into our thinking, much as any cultural vision of the universe does. It is not so much a matter of knowing or believing it is true as finding ourselves moving along within a certain world view that is conditioning our attitudes towards everything. This happens whatever culture we find ourselves working in, but here we are deliberately choosing to be carried along by a culture or view of the universe that was produced by and which continues to produce Awakened beings. The attitudes suggested by this vision tend to rub off on us very easily and in very helpful ways. In a culture in which everyone is thought to have the Awakened Heart and is supported by connections with the mandala of Awakening, it is easier to relax with confidence in the awareness practice. In a culture where all we believe in is self-effort and proving ourselves, it is hard not to either feel a failure or proud and self-satisfied - in other words, false confidence or none at all. The vast vision of Awakened beings tells us that there is far to go and that we are but on the first rungs of the ladder, as it were. It also tells us we have reason to be confident that the fruits of our practice are certain and so we do not have to constantly doubt and undermine ourselves.

The more deeply we trust that we have the fully-perfect Awakened Heart already within us, the more we can let go of anxiously striving after some kind of goal and simply relax into the reality of our awareness, in which the past, present and future interpenetrate. Even just an inkling of this kind of vision might enable us to adopt the attitude of one who has already traversed the path to Awakening and is now simply waiting to realise it. Even without the full realisation of this as truth, to have just an inkling or whiff of this being a possibility, can enable us to step out of entrenched attitudes, freeing up blocked energy and allowing deep relaxation at the same time. The combination of our direct experience of what it is like to open out into new possibilities and our confidence in those already well established on the path to Awakening, gives us confidence to open up even more. We can begin to dare to truly empathise with the vastness and depths of suffering that there is in the Universe without feeling overwhelmed or crushed by it. Until we dare to do this, we cannot bear to see too much suffering. Once we have the vision and confidence to open up, we will find that the more suffering we see, the more determined we are to pursue the path of Awakening. We can do this without becoming depressed or desperate, because our world view gives us the confidence and joy that we are actually going to be able to help every single being to arrive at complete Awakening, the end of suffering. Somehow the vastness of the vision forces us to give up our narrow ego ambitions. Awakening is of no interest or advantage to the ego mandala. There is nothing in it to grasp or own. The Endless Compassionate Vision of being dedicated to helping and Awakening others is the end of all our egocentric ambitions for self-aggrandisement.

Activities that help us to deepen our understanding of the nature of being:

Reviewing sections in 'Discovering the Heart of Buddhism' that suggest a vaster vision

Studying, reflecting and meditating on the vision of reality explored in 'Trusting the Heart of Buddhism'

Studying and reflecting on the principles laid down in the *Mahayana Sutra Principles* Booklet by Rigdzin Shikpo and Shenpen

Studying sutras and other traditional texts, teaching about the nature of reality

Reading or listening to stories of Awakened Beings, absorbing the world-view implicit in the stories

Making Pranidhanas

From one point of view, we only need to develop one intention. We only need to link into our deepest Heart Wish to Awaken and to Awaken others. From this point of view, simply to rest in the Awakened Heart is the most perfect way to develop the power of our intention. This is what is known as the ultimate Bodhichitta, which we have been referring to throughout as our deepest Heart Wish. The ultimate Bodhichitta (literally:- Awakened Heart) is what that experience of the Heart Wish really is. It is the living Truth, ultimate Reality itself, alive within us and which emerges as we traverse the path to Awakening. This wish is obstructed by our confusion and lack of clarity on all sorts of levels. It is also obstructed by the myriad of conflicting wishes that we harbour and foster in the mandala of our being. So there are many aspects to training our inherent power to focus our wishes and resolves in order to make them powerful and effective. On the one hand, there is training to give up conflicting wishes; on the other hand, there is training to link into the Heart Wish, the Awakened Heart, directly through formless practice.

Training to focus our wishes and intentions helps overcome the obstructions that prevent our linking into our deepest Heart Wish. Linking into our deepest Heart Wish is what the ultimate practice *is*. So it is like the chicken and the egg. Which comes first? Is it linking into our deepest Heart Wish or removing the obstructions to doing this? We cannot remove the obstructions to linking into it until we have linked into it, but linking into it is the result of removing the obstructions!

So there is a kind of play going on here, as is always the case when we get to the real heart of the Dharma. We have to find within ourselves the way to activate the Heart Wish and, once activated, it works for us to remove all obstructions and fulfil all our wishes. On the one hand, we have to make a contrived effort to activate the Heart Wish and specify what we are resolving to bring about. On the other hand, we have to let go and trust the Heart Wish to spontaneously bring this about without our ego-grasping effort.

The Heart Wish is the longing in our heart of hearts. It longs in an unformulated way for happiness, the Truth, the end of suffering or at least some sense of relief. When we trace each one of our wishes, volitions, intentions or choices back to its root, it is always springing from this deep wish for happiness or satisfaction. Even the most distorted form of behaviour has this wish as its root, and is some desperate attempt to squeeze some trickle of satisfaction out of the universe. Why is this so? It is because it is the very nature of our being and the root of our behaviour, and so of our experience. It is the very nature of awareness itself to long for satisfaction and joy. This is what drives us on the path to Awakening. It is also what drives samsara.

Ultimately, the Heart Wish is our innate sensitivity and responsiveness searching for its own nature, which expresses itself as a sense of well-being. The Heart Wish is our power of choice, of volition, of wishing that creates all the worlds that we enter. It is this power that, when distorted, creates the karmic worlds that we get born into again and again. It is this power that takes us on the merry-go-round of our thinking processes when we sit to meditate. It is always with us. When undistorted and fully operative, it is what propels us along the path to Awakening, and eventually flowers as the pranidhanas of Awakened beings that can create whole worlds for the benefit of others.

This power we have is important right from the start of the path, because it is a fundamental aspect of the nature of awareness to be able to take up a direction, to flow in a particular direction. This is what is happening when we build up good or bad habits and find ourselves repeatedly experiencing the same kinds of situations. The direction is always determined by a movement in our awareness, which we might call volition or choice. So having linked into our deepest heart wish, we find that our volitions and choices emanate from that place, but they take on particular shapes and they flow in particular directions. It is this power that we use when we decide we are going to meditate for half an hour every day, or follow the path to Awakening. It is the same power, when it has fully emerged, that enables Awakened beings to create

Pure Lands for other beings to enter and be drawn to Awakening.

In our own small way, we use this power to make resolves like 'I will never make that mistake again' or 'I am going to stick with this until I really understand it'. Later on, we may find ourselves enjoying the good fortune of being able to settle easily and naturally into meditation, or find ourselves in a really good Dharma situation and wonder why. Often, it can be traced back to having had this kind of resolve, sometimes quite inexplicably, from earliest childhood. From the perspective of the Buddhist path, such happy circumstances did not just arise from nowhere, but from the power of our previous resolves that are somehow still impelling us forward in a certain direction.

The more we appreciate the fact that our resolves do have a power, even when we have forgotten we ever made them, the more eager we are to make and reinforce resolves at every possible opportunity. One way of doing this is to rejoice in resolves we have already made and which others have made. So when we see someone enjoying the kind of good fortune we long for - when, for example, we see someone able to follow the path to awakening without obstacles, we can think that this arose from their previous resolves. Taking this as an example of how resolves do really bear fruit, we can rejoice to see their good fortune and make the same resolves as they made. 'May I make the same resolves as they have, so that I can follow the path to Awakening as they do.' Thinking like this, instead of feeling discouraged and even envious of others who are more advanced on the path than we are, we use their example for our own practice. Our rejoicing in the success of their resolve becomes our own practice in the sense that we make the same resolve, so that we will reap the same fruit.

Strengthening our resolves in this way, as we bring them in line with our heart wish, is something we can do at any time. However negative and distracting our life may be at times, we can use those times to strengthen our resolve. This is practice. You do not have to wait until your life circumstances change before you start to practise. You start right there in the difficult situation by making resolves. Times like that are excellent opportunities to strengthen our resolve and rejoice at the strength of our resolve and the resolve of others who have shown us the way.

Making resolves in this way is what firms up as our shila, our conduct that is in line with this resolve. The resolve can be firmed up as a vow or one's word of honour. By reinforcing our resolves and seeing how they bear fruit, our confidence in the power of our word and integrity increases and eventually we are able to make the same pranidhanas as the Bodhisattvas have done in the past for the vast benefit of others. In the meantime, it is our power of resolve that enables us to follow the path to Awakening.

You can think of resolve in this sense as a firming up of our motivation. Once the resolve is set in motion, it becomes our motivation even when we are not particularly thinking about it. For example, you might resolve to follow the path to Awakening and then find yourself going along to a Dharma talk. You may not actually think to yourself 'I am going to the Dharma talk, because I want to follow the path to Awakening'. You may just think 'Oh, that looks like an interesting talk', but actually what is really motivating you is a deep inner resolve to do all you can to follow the path to Awakening. It is as if your resolves from the past have become an inherent part of you, determining what you like and dislike, what you choose to do and how you respond to things. All this depends on our resolves of the past and our future depends on our resolves of the present.

You could think that resolves are really the same thing as strengthening our good tendencies, but by calling it our power of resolve, we are emphasising that it is a power inherent in our awareness and something we have immediate access to. It also emphasises the importance of the connection between our heart wish and our power of resolve. It is not so much a mechanical process of cause and effect, but more a creative process emanating from the true nature of our awareness and from the depths of our heart.

At the moment, we do not understand just what an incredible power of creativity there is in awareness. But after we have absorbed the vision revealed to us in the Buddhist tradition, and our view of reality has begun to be changed by our experience in meditation, we might begin to understand how it is that Awakened beings, by focusing their wishes as pranidhanas, can bring about actual changes in the, seemingly, external world. In fact, they can create whole worlds, that others can enter and in which they can be taught the path to Awakening. It becomes more and more meaningful for us to make pranidhanas with confidence as the Awakened beings of the past did, those of the present do and as all those of the future will do. We can confidently recite the pranidhanas handed down to us in the Buddhist tradition as examples of the pranidhanas of Awakened beings, thereby training in making pranidhanas for ourselves, as well as linking into the pranidhanas that they have already made.

Activities that support our developing the power and purity of our intention include:

Returning again and again to the sections in 'Discovering the Heart of Buddhism' and 'Trusting the Heart of Buddhism' on Heart Wish, honesty, confidence, being true to our word, change of heart

Reflecting on the sections in 'Trusting the Heart of Buddhism' on pranidhana

Dedicating our punya to the Awakening of all beings

Taking our wishes seriously and developing the habit of focusing them deliberately when they accord with our Heart Wish

Taking Refuge and the Bodhisattva Vow, and studying and reflecting on their meaning

Reciting the pranidhanas made by Awakened Beings so that we become one with them in our hearts and can accomplish what they have accomplished, for example the *Samantabhadracharya Pranidhana* and Rangjung Dorje's *Mahamudra Pranidhana*

Making Connections

When we talk about ultimate practice - just resting in the true nature of our being, simply recognising reality without even the subtlest form of fear or grasping - it sounds as if it is something we have to learn to do, a kind of not-doing that we have to learn to 'do'.

Although it is sometimes presented this way, it is not really a matter of learning a special trick called 'not-doing'. However long we struggled with our ego habit of grasping and trying to let go, we would never get any nearer to what is meant by 'not doing'. This is because the space of utter non-doing just happens by itself in the Openness of our being. It is as if it comes to us rather than we do it or learn to do it. So as we move along the path and we find ourselves falling or being sucked into this space of non-doing, there are forces at work within us that are totally beyond our deluded sense of being able to control things. We just have to sit back and let the process of Awakening happen, letting *it* be itself. It is a matter of our Buddha Nature awakening in us; Openness, Clarity, and Sensitivity stir within us and break asunder the chains of delusion with which we have bound them.

There is a subtle limitation to our ability to really rest in non-doing though, if we conceive of the situation as being like I've described above. This limitation arises because our idea of 'my Buddha Nature' or 'my Openness, Clarity and Sensitivity' is too limited. The problem is twofold: first, that our ego-mandala attempts to 'own' or credit to itself, as part of its kingdom, something that it is proud of, the idea of the Buddha Nature and its unfolding. The second part of the problem is that we have too narrow and limited an idea of what we are, and therefore of what our Buddha Nature is, what our awareness is and what might happen in it. Therefore, if we think that our Awakening is something that is happening within us, caused by something within us (our Buddha Nature), it is likely that we will not be able to really drop all our preconceptions and rest in non-doing, which is to rest in the Awakened Heart.

The Mahayana Buddhist tradition teaches that Openness, Clarity and Sensitivity is actually the nature of the Universe itself. It is true, up to a point, that we have only our own Openness, Clarity and Sensitivity to rely on, but actually our Buddha Nature is not some kind of isolated entity separate from the Universe and everyone else's Buddha Nature. Although we are distinct individuals, our nature is the same Openness, Clarity and Sensitivity. So as we open our hearts, as we Awaken, we are actually suffused with the Openness, Clarity and Sensitivity of the Universe. Awakening is beyond any of our usual notions of me 'in here' and the world 'out there'; our idea of what we are is infinitely too limited, and our idea of everything and everyone else is infinitely too distanced. So the Openness, Clarity and Sensitivity that, as practitioners, we see is unfolding within our hearts and waking us up, is not merely our Openness,

Clarity, Sensitivity. It is, in fact, the true nature of reality, the Awakened world, drawing us into itself.

Thinking of Awakening as something alive from its own side and coming into us enables us to open out to it in a somewhat different way. It cuts through any tendency to think of Awakening as a kind of ego success story. Rather it is truly the surrender of ego. There is nothing for the grasping mind to do. Awakening dawns from its own side and has power from its own side. This is quite wonderful, but also a tremendous shock. Instead of feeling in control of the process, we have to simply remain open and let Openness, Clarity and Sensitivity unfold, revealing a world beyond our present ideas of inside and outside, self and other, time and space.

At first, teachings like this are just ideas to us. We do not have to believe them particularly. Again it is a matter of getting a hint, whiff or inkling of another possibility, so just hearing them might be enough to enable us to open up more. As we move along the path, our old ideas of what we are and what the world is, what inside and outside mean, begin to crumble in the face of the sheer mysteriousness of our direct experience. Sometimes it is as if Awakening is coming to us and sometimes it seems to arise within us, but either way is simply a way of talking.

This power coming from the Awakened world that enters and influences us, causing Awakening to happen to us, is called adhistana in Buddhism. Adhistana is a general word for influence and possession, but in this context it refers specifically to what is coming to us from the nature of reality itself, the Awakened world. It comes to us from its own side. It is not something that we make happen. It is like a power, an influence or an infection. You could think of it even as something that we are possessed by. This adhistana is working on us all the time, but it is not until we open to it that we feel its effects. It is rather like the electricity that pervades everything, but which has no particular effect until harnessed in a current. As with love and compassion (which are actually none other than the true nature of reality, the Buddha Nature), if we do not open to them, we do not feel they are there. When we let down our defences and give up our pride, then we feel them almost as a tangible force in the world.

Adhistana works on us in all sorts of ways and on all sorts of levels. Simply to sit in Formless meditation, giving our best shot at resting in the Awakened Heart, is to open ourselves to the adhistana of Awakening. The more we relax and turn towards our experience, the more we are opening to the adhistana of Awakening. In a sense, it is seeking us out and when we sit in meditation, it is as if we were laying ourselves open to being taken over and possessed by it.

In theory all we need to do to access this adhistana is simply to open to it. Openness, Clarity and Sensitivity are our very nature, so we have the most direct connection with them we possibly could have. As they are also the nature of realty and of all beings, we are also connected, with incredible intimacy, with everything and everyone. The Awakened World is right there in our heart, never separated from us for a second, even by a hair's breadth. However, because of the limitations of our vision, we do not see it like this. We think that our heart is just our boring old heart and we know just what that is. We don't really believe that we have all these connections with Awakening and that all we need to do is open up and its adhistana will come flooding in. The fact that we are holding back and don't really believe we have these connections creates a subtle block to our being able to fully receive the adhistana. Nevertheless, just by virtue of the connections themselves, adhistana does flow to some extent, if not as fully as it would if we believed in it.

Furthermore, there is tremendous significance in the structure of our personal mandala and its connections with the world and other beings. It is not that Openness, Clarity and Sensitivity are an amorphous blob in which 'anything goes'. It is a structured mandala, albeit interpenetrated by all other mandalas. The way we are connected to other mandalas is very significant in terms of how effectively we are going to be able to communicate and work with them. Although, in the true nature of reality, we are all connected to every being (including every Awakened being) in exactly the same way - in practice, in order to be effective at any particular time and place, we need to have made the right connections. This works both ways. Awakened Beings (Bodhisattvas) do things deliberately to make connections with beings and to encourage those beings to do things that make connections with them. It is not just a matter of their making powerful pranidhanas and directing their adhistana to help all beings, but they also go to a lot of trouble to establish connections with beings so that those beings can make connections with them and also with other Awakened Beings.

Practicalities of Living the Awakened Heart

Living the Awakened Heart is Centred on Personal Guidance

Living the Awakened Heart is one's personal training within the Awakened Heart Sangha and so should not be thought of as a public or linear programme of teachings, a kind of obstacle course towards gaining credentials within some kind of educational system. Not everyone's journey will be quite that, same, so the point is not to try to conform to a standard pattern (even though conformity to the tradition has an important part to play in preserving the structure and dynamic of a teaching mandala). It is very much a matter of understanding the underlying principles and then applying them, working with your own inspiration, the guidance of a mentor, and the help of Sangha companions. Thus, the 'Living the Awakened Heart, training is not meant to be a series of different new practices to distract you from your ongoing exploration of the Awakened Heart. Instead, it presents you with various options you might at certain times choose to incorporate into your practice in order to deepen it.

What makes it a training is that, rather than just leaving you to your own devices in terms of how to follow the path to Awakening, there is personal advice and guidance from a mentor. Personal guidance is useful in all forms of learning, but is especially important when it comes to pursuing the path to Awakening. This is because, although we may stumble on the truth even without a teacher, we are unlikely to have confidence in it without a teacher to encourage us. There are so many ways in which we can get the wrong end of the stick, because it is not just a matter of learning the right words. We need to check out our experience with someone more experienced than ourselves and this has to be done in our own words and in our own way through one-to-one direct communication.

Your own inspiration that unfolds in the training may lead you to work ever more closely with a particular teacher and the nature of that teacher-student relationship may become extremely directive at times. This is something that can develop as your understanding, inspiration and relationship with a particular teacher develops. But it cannot be programmed into a training programme as if this were what was bound to happen for every student or should happen for every student. Look at the life-stories of the great yogins of the past - the way their relationship to their teachers worked out in practice varied a lot! So while personal guidance is the backbone of the 'Living the Awakened Heart' training, there is no single set pattern that the relationship should take at all times or for all people.

Extensive personal contact with me is not exactly a requirement for participating in Awakened Heart Sangha activities, but it doesn't mean very much to say that you are engaged in the 'Living the Awakened Heart' training if you are not in personal contact with either me or your Mentor. 'Living the Awakened Heart' is not a set of special activities that you can tick off your list of things to be done or learnt. Rather, it is the whole process of working with me over a sustained period of time, exploring your experience and deepening your practice under my guidance. As time goes on, I hope to train others to teach alongside me, but at the moment the whole 'Living the Awakened Heart' training involves direct (if not face to face) contact with me.

This doesn't mean that you have to take me as your only teacher or that you cannot take teachings and advice from others, especially those within the same tradition, such as Khenpo Rinpoche or Rigdzin Shikpo. The whole matter of what is meant by personal guidance from a teacher in the Buddhist tradition is deep and subtle. It is not easy to sum it up within the terms available to us in our culture. That is why I have been working for some time on a book in which I discuss as many of the relevant issues as I can, so that the reader can get a good overall sense of what are reasonable expectations to have, and assumptions to make, in regard to working with Buddhist teachers.

As far as working with me is concerned, I like students to inform me from time to time (at least two or three times a year) how their practice is going. Even if students feel nothing much has changed since last they spoke to me or that they have been failing miserably to maintain their practice, I still want them to contact me, so that at the very least they keep the relationship alive. It gives me the opportunity to give encouragement, support and reassurance, even if no real help in terms of guidance. I do not regard this as a waste of time. At least by contacting me you are making a living connection to the mandala of Awakening. Ideally, you will contact me to discuss how your practice is going, seeking my advice or simply affirmation that your practice is proceeding satisfactorily. with any luck, you will enjoy talking to me and get some inspiration out of it!

Another reason why it is important to contact me is that the meditation instructions are very personal in the sense that it is not self-evident what they mean. It is not until you ask me directly whether your understanding is right or not, that you have the opportunity to test it out. It also lets me know whether you are proceeding along the right lines or not. Sometimes you may feel you need to contact me frequently for a period of time, just to settle a particular subtle point in your practice that is not easy to talk about. I do not mind if you seem to be asking the same question again and again. Sometimes one just has to keep asking until one is really sure. Sometimes you may want to contact me every week, while at other times once a month is enough. I do not want to lay down any strict rules here. Some people contact me every two or three months and that works well.

When you contact me, I like to hear about your meditation, how much time you are able to give to it, how it is going, and any questions you have regarding it. I also like to hear what materials you are working on and how you are finding them. I am interested in things you find unclear and difficult or even things you disagree with. So please don't think you should only tell me what you think is good (although that is nice to hear too!).

The Rhythm of Living the Awakened Heart

Dharma practice, and thus 'Living the Awakened Heart', is unceasing, not something that we do only at certain limited times and places. But that does not mean our practice is a never-ending burden, that we have to it always have at the front of our r minds; rather, our practice is a mandala with a rhythm of both focused times and unfocused times. Our Dharma practice, and 'Living the Awakened Heart', is like a fire that is growing within us: the sharp and focused flickers, like tongues of flame, are the most obvious sign and lead the way, but they arise out of the pervasive and persisting heat of the fire. Unleashing a powerful fire involves working with both the flames and the heat, for they arise together inseparably. It is just the same with our Dharma practice. The formal sessions of study, contemplation or meditation arise from - but also lead and fuel - the gradual rising of the Dharma within us, imperceptibly pervading all aspects of our lives and the depths of our being. An important part of the 'Living the Awakened Heart' training is ensuring that our practice and training contain both this focused foreground and relaxed background, that we are giving space and importance to both and that they are working properly together. This dynamic of focusing and relaxing, moving from foreground to background, is the nature of awareness. In 'Discovering the Heart of Buddhism' it is introduced as the dynamic of EVAM, of E (relaxed background) and VAM (focused foreground). Learning to work with it, both in our meditation and awareness practice, and in our whole attitude to our lives and practice, is fundamental to the training. We tend to think that it is only when we are focused on our practice (only when it is really in the foreground of our awareness) that anything is happening. So it is as if, in between nothing is happening. Such an attitude is a great obstacle, both to understanding the nature of awareness in meditation and to being able to set up a powerful practice mandala.

There are many different aspects to this subject, but I want to focus mainly on two of them here. Firstly, that it is fundamental lo Dharma practice to learn to relate to relaxed unfocused ,awareness/ as this is the very space that is the ground of our being. Secondly, that it is important that we do have periods of focused practice.

Relaxed unfocused awareness is the very ground of our being; it is that space that we both long for and are terrified of. We must be careful not to use our Dharma practice as another way to distract ourselves from this great nowhereness that is right under our noses and that we are trying to deny. It is important to value those in-between moments, those moments when we might just be staring out of the window or when we suddenly switch focus. That is also awareness. It is the background awareness out of which everything else springs and in which everything else has its existence. Once we realise that this relaxed aspect of awareness is important and always present, then we can understand how it might be possible to cultivate continuity of practice. we can keep returning to awareness practice by treating gaps as aspects of awareness itself, rather than as dead space.

So learning to relate to what seem like gaps in awareness is absolutely essential to deepening our practice and to developing the confidence to rest in the unbroken continuity of awareness. By turning towards these gaps with relaxed confidence, again and again, our whole view of what they are changes. We begin to see that awareness is unbroken, that it is always there without any holes at all. What we call Saps are unfocused, background moments in the Openness or 'nowhereness' of experience, the indestructible ground of our being in which we are developing confidence.

So in our everyday life it is good to notice those anxious moments when we think we are wasting time. Maybe you have to wait for the computer to boot up, or the phone to ring, someone to finish speaking, or the train to start, or whatever it is' By noticing the anxiety or pressure to get on to the next thing or to fill up the gap, we can turn towards it and notice that this too is awareness. There is no break in awareness. So in this sense there is no such thing as wasted time. Appreciate the spaciousness of those moments, *u\"p into them and relax.

By noticing the impulse to fill up every moment so that there are no gaps (the disease of our age), we could let it go sometimes. Instead, we could start programming gaps into our day. For example, instead of leaving it to the last minute to get to appointments, you could aim to get there early so that you have to wait around for a bit and then really relax into that gap.

It is tempting to try to fill up our whole Dharma life, rushing from one thing to the next, as if VAM, VAM, VAM was what it was all about. Sometimes, especially in our society, we have so many ideas about what we should be doing with our time that we feel almost guilty to stop. Somehow we should be trying to achieve something, get something, improve or fix something. Just to relax and do nothing seems like a sign of failure. We easily carry this attitude over into our Dharma practice and we start to feel that this is yet another thing we should be filling up our time with, yet another thing to do, or to fail to do. It is yet another source of pressure. So it is important to think that the longed for gaps, when there is no pressure, are your Dharma practice. They are important and are, in themselves, awareness. You don't have to do anything to them. They are perfect awareness in themselves. You just need to notice and have confidence in them.

Tibetan teachers often talk about not being distracted, not wasting a moment. But this doesn't mean that our practice should be constant effort and pressure. It doesn't mean it should be VAM, VAM, VAM and no E. The important point here is to recognise the need to develop a sense of on-going practice through both the background, unfocused E periods and strong focused VAM moments. For example, when the time comes to die or at moments of deepest suffering, it might simply be a background sense of confidence in the nature of awareness that sustains us, even though our thoughts and feelings are in turmoil.

It is possible to structure our daily life in such a way that we nurture confidence in the simplicity of the awareness practice at all times, remembering to keep coming back to it in a focused way as often as possible. We not only need to cultivate the focus of foreground awareness, but also to make sure we have confidence in and respect the background awareness at the same time. We cannot learn to rest in our true nature by rushing around trying, struggling and pushing to keep focused on the foreground. If we remain simple and relaxed, the E and the VAM (the movement from foreground to background) occurs naturally and we can rest in it with confidence. As soon as we lose this simplicity and try to make awareness be as we think it should be, we interfere with the naturalness of the EVAM, either getting lost in the background or struggling with the foreground. You may find that you need to make it part of your daily, weekly or annual routine to put time aside to relax. This might take quite ! lot of care, since the temptation might be to take time off to' d\o' something else. In other words, you simply extend the old pattern by just changing the name of what you are doing. There should be times in which you are not latching onto some kind of distracting entertainment, not trying to accomplish some kind of goal, not guiltily feeling you should be doing something else. Depending on who you are, you may find this the most challenging part of your practice of all!

It is more a way of being than a matter of what you actually do. It may be the way you sit down and drink a cup of tea. It may be the way you go and potter in the garden or water the flowers. It may be the way you lie in bed at night before you go to sleep or in the morning when you wake up. So often we spend our time counting up and measuring, comparing and worrying about what we have and have not accomplished. However, in the end, the practice is to simply *be*. It is totally irrelevant what we have and have not accomplished. Our only purpose is to accomplish the benefit of others and the best way to do that is to learn to just be.

This does not mean we should make no effort to practise awareness. To maintain our inspiration we do need to make the effort to commit ourselves to regular and sustained meditation and daily life awareness practice. It is crucial to have focused points, such as meditation sessions and Sangha events, because until we are very far along the path, our practice will weaken and crumble without them.

Our meditation sessions and those times when we come together as a Sangha are focused moments for energising our practice mandala. They are points of focus, when the Dharma is brought into the foreground, it then moves into the background as we get on with our lives. It is still there and surfaces from time to time. Even while in the background, something is happening. The energy of the focused movement pervades our background awareness in a relaxed way.

We can also arrange to create little moments of VAM at frequent intervals throughout the dry. One way to do this is to remember what is suggested in 'Discovering the Heart of Buddhism', which is to notice times in the day when you have a little gap, such as when you stop for a coffee break, travel to work, step out of the house, get into the car, brush your teeth, go to the toilet and so on. Make up your mind to make these gaps 'triggers of awareness', so that your mind starts to associate those moments with coming back to the practice in a focused way. They are moments for remembering that, even during the times when we are not very focused, everything is still going on in awareness. Awareness is always present without a break.

It is also good to observe VAM times on a larger cycle, such as special days. The full-moon day of each month is thought of as a special time in the Buddhist tradition. You could make this into a regular VAM moment by always doing a bit extra meditation practice and / o, some piece of liturgy. If it is not possible on the actual full-moon day, maybe you could choose a weekend day that is close to it. We can also have VAM places, special places or situations where we come to practice. The most obvious possibility is a shrine or a special place for meditation that you set up in your house (details of how to do this are in the booklet 'Mandala of Sacred Space'). Going to a retreat or teachings are also like this.

In conclusion, it is a vital part of our awareness practice to really value both the E and VAM aspects of awareness, and we can train to do this with both the attitudes we apply in our meditation sessions, and the attitudes we have to the practice in our whole lives. We need to make sure that in our practice we work with both E and VAM, developing a sense that our awareness practice continues without interruption in a rhythm of sharp focus, foreground and spacious, relaxed confidence, background. We need to make sure that we nurture and intensify the VAM aspect of practice, and that we do not get lost in or reject the E aspect. E and VAM are inseparable , and. unless we work with both of them we will not be able to find the right touch. We would do well to remember the story of the musician in the life of the Buddha. The Buddha told him to fine tune his meditation as he would a lute string to get the right sound. The E and the VAM are like the engine of our practice mandala that needs to be fine-tuned in order to propel us forward on the path.

Living the Awakened Heart in your Daily Life

Daily Routine

It is important to have a daily routine, even if it is quite minimal because, without it, it is very easy for days, weeks, months or even years to slip by without having maintained contact with the practice. For many of us there are so many demands on our time and energy that it is just too easy to think that we will do the practice later, when we have time, only to find that the day never seems to come. On the other hand, if we daily do certain actions without fail, somehow that pattern establishes itself as part of our being. That pattern will tend to draw us back to the practice of awareness and the path of Awakening, reminding us of what our true values are and what our life is really about. You may like to consult with me about setting up a daily routine that is suitable for you.

An ideal daily routine for someone living an ordinary working lifestyle might be to meditate an hour in the morning and an hour in the evening, spending half an hour a day looking at course materials and perhaps listening to tapes of teachings. With this as a basis one might find several slots during the day where one could do walking meditation or simply sit and reflect on some point or exercise that you have been focusing on.

However, many or most people don't have this kind of time available. It may be that we need to think about the relative importance of all our activities and, perhaps, cut down on some of them, in order to devote more time to meditation. It may be that for the present we have no option. The important thing is to keep the aspiration alive to find more time for meditation so that when the opportunities do arise we are ready for them. In the meantime, by keeping up the practice, even if only for a few brief periods each day, it is much easier to start extending the periods at the first opportunity. In fact, the practice inspires us to find more time. It is important to set up a daily schedule of practice, even if you are too busy to set aside long periods of meditation or hardly any meditation periods at all. If we let it slip, thinking 'It's no good unless I can do a whole hour' , for example, the tendency is to make such a big thing of it that we build up a resistance to the practice and never do even five minutes.

At the very least, if you're serious about the training you should set and keep to the aim of meditating for five minutes three times a day. Most people can manage five minutes when they wake up, five minutes during the day, or maybe during the evening and five minutes before going to sleep at night. Even if this is all one can do for long periods of one's life, it is immensely better than letting the practice slip all together. Here are some suggestions for things you could incorporate into a daily schedule. You might find that just one or two of these suggestions make a big difference to the way you live your life:

Remember the heart wish as soon as you wake up, and think that your every movement of body, speech and mind during the day are for the purpose of Awakening. (For this you may like to use the liturgy called 'Turning the Mind Away from Samsara'). Make an offering of a candle or incense on a shrine. I have written a booklet 'Mandala of Sacred Space' that tells you the traditional manner of setting up and relating to a shrine.

Sit and reflect, recite liturgy and meditate for a set period of time

Decide on what you are going to use as triggers of awareness throughout the day.

If you have been introduced to a mantra, you could recite it from time to time during the day when you have some free moments.

Do offering liturgy at meals or at least mentally offer your food.

Before going to sleep, remember the good you have done, feel pleased and dedicate it to the Awakening of all beings. Regret the bad and resolve not to do it in future. Think as you drop off to sleep that this might be your last sleep. Death may come before you wake. Practise having the same confidence that you want to have at the time of death. Be prepared to die at any time.

Generally speaking, everything you do in the course of your day that is in line with right conduct of body, speech and mind is Dharma practice. The more we bring all our actions of body, speech and mind into line with the path to Awakening, the more effective our Dharma practice is.

Periods of Increased Practice

It is good to put aside a period each week when you read carefully and reflect on the course materials (if you can't do this more often), or do extra meditation.

Traditionally, the full-moon is thought of as a very auspicious and powerful time and so it is good to do extra practice on that day (or the nearest day to it that you can manage). These days, now that we do not organise our lives in phase with the moon, you may find it works better to choose one or two days each month to particularly devote to practice. Such special days are a good time to do feast offerings. If you have practices that you like to do, but do not have time to do them every day, you could decide to do them on full-moon or other special days. Such practices might include the Heart Sutra, Shakyamuni and Guru Rinpoche prayers, mantras and pranidhanas such as the Samantabhadracharya Pranidhana or the Mahamudra Pranidhana of the Third Karmapa., Rangjung Dorje, that Khenpo Rinpoche taught us.

Other traditional times that are good for all these activities are Guru Rinpoche day (10th day of the Tibetan month), Dakini Day (25th of the Tibetan month) and the new moon (last day of the Tibetan month). Dates can be obtained from the Rigpa Diary available from Zam Trading.

It is good to put aside at least a few days each year for retreat, either at a group retreat or simply on your own. The Hermitage of the Awakened Heart is a place dedicated to retreat, where you can come to do solitary retreat and where I am available to give guidance during your retreat. If you do it on your own, it is still good to ask me for a retreat programme and advice. Ask the office how you can get a handout about how to set up a retreat, and also ask for details about the Hermitage.

Reading

Some people like to read books on Buddhism outside of the reading that I have suggested at the end of each section. Although there is much to be gained from reading life stories, sutras and songs of inspiration as an integral part of one's practice, this is more than just reading.

When people ask me what they should read in general, I find it very hard to know what to suggest, because people read for different reasons. I do not think it is particularly necessary or useful to read lots of books on Buddhism but, if people are in the habit of reading anyway, I suppose it is all right. The problem is that there are very few books on Buddhism that I could recommend without reservation. They all tend to use terminology differently and, even if not wrong, they make points that need further explanation. I would prefer people to use their time simply to reflect on the course work and their direct experience.

This is not to say that there is no value in trying to get a good intellectual background concerning the whole tradition, in order to understand the context of the way we teach in the Awakened Heart Sangha. I do not think this is necessary for one's practice though.

Having said this, you can find a comprehensive list of all the books I recommend in your Personal Pathway folder materials. If you haven't received this and would like a copy please email the office.

Intensive Training in Meditation and Study

Although I have already referred to reading, I consider study to be in a different category. By study I mean looking at specific texts or topics and discussing them with me and your Mentors to make sure that your understanding is developing in the right way. I will be running intensive study courses at the Hermitage of the Awakened Heart together with meditation for periods of months or even years at a time. I suggest, if you would be interested in this kind of programme were it available, that you speak to me about it. The courses that I teach at the Hermitage are recorded and we are building up packages of teaching materials on various aspects of the training. These will be made available to all my Members who want to deepen their practice in this way.

Living the Awakened Heart within the Sangha

Teaching events like weekends and retreats are wonderful opportunities in many ways. Of course, first and foremost, they are an opportunity to experience the live transmission of the teachings from teachers. They are also an opportunity to support and engage in the whole event, both for the sake of oneself and others. It is an opportunity to meet other Sangha members, to be inspired or irritated by them! This can only be stimulating for your own practice while, at the same time, your presence can be the same for others. This takes place not only in the discussion groups, but also in the breaks, as well as in the whole process of working together to make the event as pleasant as possible for all concerned.

Recitation of liturgy and meditation together in a group has a very powerful effect. It creates a sacred space that we all share in and this communicates itself at a deep level, in a way that is hard to express in words. Having practised together in a group, simply remembering the group when practising on your own can be very strengthening and reassuring.

Generally speaking, the weekends and retreats are opportunities to go more deeply into the teachings, particularly themes from the 'Discovering the Heart of Buddhism' and 'Trusting the Heart of Buddhism' courses. The themes themselves can be explored by working with the course materials and cassettes, but because the teachings are live, there is always something fresh and new emerging. Sometimes it is hard to say why hearing a certain teaching at a certain time caused the penny to drop when, in fact you think about it, you realise you have heard it many times and known it for a long time. It is something to do with the way connections and adhistana come together. It can seem quite magical sometimes.

So although Sangha events are not strictly necessary for everyone, they are immensely valuable and some people find that they are what keeps them going more than anything else. Of course, it is better if it is our own meditation and awareness practice that really keeps us going, since it is only our own practice that is with us all the time and with us when we die. Nevertheless, whatever we do that keeps us inspired is part of the path to Awakening and so is good to do.

I classify teaching events as either 'Heart of Awakening' or 'Vaster Vision'. To put it in a nutshell, the 'Heart of Awakening' events are the core of the training for everyone, regardless of how long they have been practising. They focus on different aspects of Formless meditation practice and daily life awareness, drawing attention to subtleties and difficulties and their implication in terms of our life and practice. The 'Vaster Vision' events are likely to include more technicalities concerning the Buddhist view of the Universe and its implications in terms of our practice. This kind of teaching is for deepening our understanding of the core 'Heart of Awakening' material, but may not be to everyone's taste.

Although I teach this Vaster Vision to deepen your understanding of the same essential points introduced in Heart of Awakening events, it is not always immediately obvious how this relates to the simplicity of our direct experience and may involve reference to some Buddhist jargon and terminology with which you may be unfamiliar. The vaster vision offered by the Buddhist tradition can be tremendously helpful for our meditation and daily life awareness practice, and it's especially important when it comes to thinking about the time of death and how to relate to that.

I regard the themes in Heart of Awakening as essential for everyone and the Vaster Vision themes as optional extras that might help some people go deeper into their experience and understanding of the essential points, but which might simply alienate or distract others. It is important for the Sangha as a whole that people be mainly interested in deepening their experience of the essential points, which are most directly dealt with at Heart of Awakening events you may be wondering how this distinction between Heart of Awakening and Vaster Vision relates to the difference between 'Discovering the Heart of Buddhism' and 'Trusting the Heart of Buddhism'. There is a relationship: Heart of Awakening events focus very much on the exploration of our direct experience, in the same way that 'Discovering the Heart of Buddhism' does. So you could say the Heart of Awakening and 'Discovering the Heart of Buddhism' share the same flavour, while the Vaster Vision events are more related to 'Trusting the Heart of Buddhism'. However, both Heart of Awakening and (particularly) Vaster Vision events can introduce specific material, or ways of expressing things, that are not elaborated in either of 'Discovering the Heart of Buddhism' or 'Trusting the Heart of Buddhism'.

There is a very important reason why we don't call these events 'Discovering the Heart of Buddhism' events rather than Heart of Awakening events and 'Trusting the Heart of Buddhism' events rather than Vaster Vision events. This is that the Heart of Awakening events are the core events for everyone, whether they are working on 'Discovering the Heart of Buddhism' for the first time or are working on, or have in the past worked on, 'Trusting the Heart of

Buddhism'. Similarly, Vaster Vision events are open to everyone who finds them helpful.

As for advice about which events in the annual programme you should choose to come to, for many people it is simply a question of time and availability. In other words, they come to events that fall on dates when they are free to come, even though parts of a Vaster Vision event might be a bit over their heads. This does not have to be a problem and there is always a lot you can learn, even if you don't get all of it. If you have the option and would like more advice about which events would be best for you, then this is something you could talk to me about.

Annual Sangha Celebration

I encourage the whole Awakened Heart Sangha to treat the Annual Sangha Celebration, which is held at the Hermitage each year, as a special occasion. Even if you cannot make it to the weekend, you can still be with us all in spirit. At the Annual Sangha Celebration, we have a feast offering puja and it is an opportunity for people to strengthen their practice by taking Refuge or the Bodhisattva vow and/or rejoicing with those who are doing so. It is also a time for remembering those who have died during the year and thinking about how fleeting life is and how important the Dharma is when we die.

Supporting practices of Living the Awakened Heart

You can read an overview of training in the Awakened Heart in *A Lifetime of Practice.*

There are various courses and practices that form the body of our common practice and training together in the Awakened Heart Sangha. It is not that everyone has to engage in all of these things, but rather that these are all done publicly and are commonly talked about. They are the common ground we all share, as opposed to other practices that from time to time I may advise certain individual students to do, but which I don't publicly talk about to the Sangha as a whole.

These activities are all for the purpose of supporting our essential practice of exploring our awareness and seeking to rest in our true nature. They are a rich set of supports, and provide all the structure that many people will need for a lifetime of deep Dharma practice.

Basic Liturgy

Liturgy refers to the recitations or chants that we do when we come together to meditate and so on. Buddhist liturgy always includes the taking of Refuge and the Bodhisattva vow and usually includes words in praise of the Buddha, the path or truth of Awakening, and those who teach it. When you come to

Awakened Heart Sangha events, you encounter our basic liturgy, which we always use to begin and end the meditation and teaching sessions. There is also liturgy for offering food at mealtimes and for finishing meals. There are tapes that explain this entire liturgy and there are several booklets. Once you have joined in with the liturgy at an Awakened Heart Sangha event, if you feel inspired to do so, you can do it at home by yourself. If you have never attended such an event, it is possible to ask me to introduce you to the liturgy.

As much as possible, we try to keep to the tradition of passing such things on through a formal living connection, rather than people picking them up from just anywhere. It is more powerful that way. Sometimes, I may suggest that you do a practice', such as the liturgy, on your own, as a kind of inspiration with the aspiration to link into it more fully as soon as you get the opportunity to receive transmission and teaching on it.

Heart Sutra

The Heart Sutra is an important scripture within the Mahayana Buddhist tradition. This short sutra encapsulates the essence of the teachings, in a discourse delivered in the presence of the Buddha. We recite the Heart Sutra together on retreats and from time to time I give some explanations on it. Once you have joined in with the Heart Sutra at an Awakened Heart Sangha event, If you feel inspired to do so, you can do it at home by yours elf, in which case it would be good to listen to tapes giving explanations on it. If you have never attended such an event, it is possible to ask me to introduce you to it.

Mantra

A mantra is a short proclamation, such as a name of an Awakened being, the fundamental purpose of which is to link our hearts and minds into the essence of the Awakened Heart of all the Buddhas. By our repeating the sounds of the mantra/ we eventually link into the truth or reality from which all the Buddhas emanate. In the meantime, simply to repeat the mantra protects the mind (mantra literally means 'mind protection'). It protects us by keeping the mind from wandering off to negative or unhelpful mind states. It protects us much as any reminder to practice protects us. At its deepest level, it protects by means of the connection to the mandala of Awakening and the adhistana of that. How strongly it works in that sense, depends on how deeply it connects to our heart. Within the Buddhist tradition there is a great wealth of mantras and I have chosen the mantra from the Heart Sutra, the Shakyamuni mantra and the Guru Rinpoche mantra as the main mantras that we recite together as a Sangha. The Heart Sutra mantra is the mantra of the living Dharma itself and it can be repeated at any time as a way of connecting to the power of the Dharma in the heart. Similarly the Shakyamuni mantra is the mantra of the historical

Buddha, the Buddha we all feel connected to because we can trace a direct historical connection from the present dry back to him and his teachings. Guru Rinpoche (Padmasambhava) is the embodiment of our own particular lineage of teachers in the Dzogchen and Mahamudra tradition and so we feel a particularly strong sense of his presence in the teachings we receive and practices we do. If you have joined in the recitation of a mantra at a Sangha event, you can then practise the mantra whenever you feel inspired to do so. If you have never been present at an event where a particular mantra was being recited you can, if you like, ask me to introduce you to it on an individual basis.

In essence, all mantras emanating from the Awakened Heart are the same, so that we only have to do one in order to invoke the power of them all. Nonetheless, some people find they like to repeat one mantra more than another. Some people do not find it helpful to recite mantras at all. So I leave it up to each person's own inspiration. From time to time I give teachings on mantra recitation and give a transmission of a mantra. If you feel you would like to do so, you can ask me for the transmission of a mantra at any time and then recite it whenever you feel inspired to do so. There are some cassettes containing teachings on mantra recitation.

If after consultation with me you start to do mantra practice of a certain amount, then it is a good idea to get a mala (rosary) of 108 beads and to think that as you turn the beads the adhistana of the mantra enters the mala. The mala should then be treated with care as a sacred object.

Songs of Inspiration

A wonderful source of inspiration is to sing yogic songs of realisation, such as the songs of Milarepa, Guru Rinpoche and Gotsangpa that Khenpo Rinpoche has taught us over the years. Singing songs in this way brings joy to the heart and a sense of a living connection with the realisation of the lineage. It can be very moving, expressing our great yearning for truth and understanding in the face of the terrible sufferings of samsara. Sometimes, singing in this way may help us feel that the suffering is less of a burden, lightening our hearts and bringing us courage. These songs can be sung at any time, just as a way of inspiring ourselves. We hope over time to find our own translations and melodies for these songs. If you are interested in this project, you could speak to me about it.

Other possibilities

As time goes on, I introduce further stages of shamatha (peaceful abiding, Tib. *shinay*) and vipashyana (insight into truth, Tib. *hlagtong* to students, as I see fit in the course of our ongoing discussions about their Formless meditation.

The principles of Guru Yoga are present in my teaching about the living truth and are implied throughout the liturgy for those who are open and ready for such an approach. I am producing a book on Guru-student relationship and the issues surrounding the whole idea of a teacher in Buddhism.

The same is true of sadhana practice. Sadhana is about linking into the world of Awakening by using a particular mandala form. I do not intend to introduce any specific sadhana practices until I feel confident that students will benefit from them. I have introduced, enough liturgy to cover all the essential points of sadhana practice. There are so many sadhana practice texts to choose from, which involve approaching, worshipping, receiving adhistana and uniting with the living truth as expressed in a multitude of forms. However, the essence of all of them is in their mantras and even more so in the practice of resting in the Awakened Heart. With our liturgy and mantras you have the essential points of the development stage (*kyerim*) and with the Formless practice you have the essential point of the dissolving stage (*dzogrim*). There are endless details in a full traditional sadhana that go over and above the essentials. People vary and, for some, these details may be a way into the essentials. I think this is true for many Tibetans. For me and, in my experience, for most Westerners, too many details in regard to a full traditional sadhana liturgy can be more a distraction than a way into the real nature and power of the practice and can wait for much later (if indeed they are ever helpful at all).

You may be wondering why I do not make any specific mention of the 'Preliminaries' that are so often referred to in texts coming from the Tibetan tradition. The reason I do not refer to them as a particular practice is that what are referred to as 'Preliminaries' are in fact a particular form that has appeared as a relatively late development in the Buddhist tradition. However, in principle, the elements contained in them have always been practised in some form or other and are covered in the standard practice programme within the Awakened Heart Sangha. If you want to raise the matter with me, we could discuss in more detail what those elements are and whether you, as an individual, wish to concentrate on some of those elements more strongly from time to time. For example, at some point I might think it would be helpful for a particular person to do 100,000 full prostrations. For others, simply to bow to the shrine once or twice a day might be enough. We will have to see, as time goes on, how people's practice goes and what they find helpful or inspiring.

In general, when speaking to students on an individual basis, I might think a particular practice would be right for them and even suggest it to them or they might wish to ask me about a particular practice that they have heard me mention or read about. However, to introduce and talk about all sorts of different teachings at public events would only serve to confuse the basic message about resting in the Awakened Heart. This is a message hard enough to keep in focus without deliberately introducing distractions. Also, human psychology being what it is, once something new and special is mentioned, people want it just out of curiosity, whether it is useful or not. It feeds into the upwards and onwards psychology of our age. I don't want this to happen and only intend to give further practices to students who show a serious commitment to Formless Meditation, and only as a way to help them link more deeply into the Formless Meditation, the quest to rest in the Awakened Heart.

Glossary

Abhisheka (Sanskrit, Tib. *wong* or *wongkur*) often translated as 'empowerment' or 'initiation'. It has become the custom over the centuries for Tibetan teachers to offer ceremonies called 'abhisheka' as an opportunity for all-comers to receive adhistana, or as a permission or transmission for doing various visualisation and mantra practices. This is actually a misuse of the term 'abhisheka'. To understand its real meaning one needs a deep and vast understanding of the Mahayana vision, which is why I teach that before introducing any talk of abhisheka. A short definition is not really of any help here.

Adhistana (Sanskrit, Tib. chin lab), literally 'influence' or 'possession', often translated as 'blessing' or, 'grace'. It is the power that flows out from something. The most powerful and most beneficial source of adhistana is the Truth itself . See the section on 'Training in strengthening our connections to the mandala of Awakening' on this subject.

Apramanas (Sanskrit Tib: tse me shi). The Four Immeasurables (also known as the Four Brahma Viharas) which are measureless love, compassion, joy and equalness.

Avidya (Sanskrit, Tib. ma rigpa) literally, 'non-awareness', often translated as 'ignorance'. It refers to the fundamental state of not recognising our true nature, that keeps us in the state of confusion and grasping at the unreal as real. It is the cause of all suffering.

Bodhisattva (Sanskrit, Tib. chang chub sempa). Someone with the determination to awaken to full Buddhahood. Technically it refers to beings on the Bodhisattva bhumis who have realized emptiness/ met the Buddhas face to face and made the Bodhisattva vow in their presence. Less technically, it is used for anyone who aspires to follow the Bodhisattva path and has made a formal commitment to do so.

Bodhisattva Vow. In a general way it is the vow to follow the path to Awakening for the sake of others rather than just for oneself . Technically, it is the vow to realise full Buddhahood in order to work forever to liberate all beings and bring them to the same stage of perfection. It involves also taking a vow to train and to accomplish all the deeds of the Bodhisattvas for the benefit of beings. See the booklet "Taking the Bodhisattva Vow" booklet for more on this subject.

Dharma (Sanskrit, Tib. cho). Dharma is used to mean Truth or Reality with the understanding that it is what the Buddha discovered when he Awakened and then taught, revealed and demonstrated to others. It has come to be used synonymously with the path to Awakening, so we talk of practising Dharma, meaning following the path to Awakening. But since it also means the Truth revealed at Awakening, the living Truth of the Universe that is drawing us to itself, we also talk of Dharma as a force in its own right, rather than simply a path that we follow.

Dzogchen (Tibetan, Sanskrit (supposedly) atiyoga), literally 'great perfection' or 'great completion' or 'great finishing'. A term from the Nyingma or old school of Tibetan Buddhism that arrived in Tibet with Guru Rinpoche if not before. It is the name of the highest possible realization beyond even the notion of Awakened and Unawakened. It is another name for Truth or Reality itself. It is often used as if it were the name for a practice e.g. practising Dzogchen. This is a loose way of talking about practising in a way that will lead to the realisation of Dzogchen. When the Dzogchen tradition is referred to, it means the teachings coming from the lineage of teachers who have realised Dzogchen. It has its own traditions, techniques, use of technical terminology, transmissions and so on. Although it is principally thought of as the Nyingma tradition, yogins from other lineages, especially the Kagyupas also practice and transmit it.

Mahamudra (Sanskrit, Tib. chagchen) literally 'Great Seal in Tibetan. Although it is a term used in the Dzogchen tradition for a level of realisation that falls short of Dzogchen, it is used by the Kagyu tradition, synonymously with Dzogchen, for Reality or Awakening itself. This has led to endless discussions about whether Dzogchen and Mahamudra are the same or not. The third Karmapa (Rangjung Dorje, 14th century), who was one of the teachers of Longchenpa, unified the Kagyu Mahamudra and the Nyingma Dzogchen traditions into one system. So

Kagyupas tend to say Dzogchen and Mahamudra are the same.

Mahayana (Sanskrit, Tib.   tekpa chenpo), literally 'great vehicle'.   The Buddhist teachings that lead to complete and perfect Buddhahood. Mahayana sutras refer to themselves as Mahayana and contrast that with teachings that lead to a goal less than complete and perfect Buddhahood. The main issue here is that it is possible to Awaken to a kind of Enlightenment that does not realise the whole of reality and specifically it does not realise the Buddha nature that enables us to develop all the powers of a fully Awakened Buddha. These powers are of no use to ourselves but of immense benefit to others. That is why the Bodhisattva vows to attain them.

Mandala (Sanskrit, Tib.   khyil khor), literally 'centre and periphery' in Tibetan. Any structure with a centre and periphery.   Anything that appears in our awareness takes the form of a mandala consisting of a central focus and what surrounds it. Mandalas have a structure and dynamic in the sense that they are held together by connections between centre and periphery, with emotionality at the boundaries and where one mandala touches on another.   In most contexts one can substitute for mandala 'world' , ds used in the metaphorical sense. For example, we talk of the world of our experience, our social world, our psychological world, our whole world collapsing.

Pranidhana (Sanskrit, Tib. mon lam), often translated rather inadequately as 'wishing prayer' .   It is more powerful than just a wish, although it is essentially the power of our volition empowered and made effective. It is not really a prayer so much as a clearly formulated blessing or curse. When somebody powerful utters their word of truth with one pointed concentration and conviction, this is a pranidhana and it has the power to fulfil itself. For example, 'May you be well!', 'May the gods go with you!', 'May I gain Enlightenment for the sake of all beings!' See the section on 'Training in developing the power of our intention' for more on this subject.

Refuge. 'Taking refuge' is the commitment to follow the path and teachings revealed by the Buddha. It can be done informally through reciting a formal liturgy or simply being committed to the Truth and the path to Awakening. When it is taken formally at a ceremony from a preceptor, it marks a definite decision and moment of being received within the community of followers of the Buddha. See the booklet 'Taking Refuge' for more on this subject.

Sadhana (Sanskrit, Tib. drub tab) literally 'means for attainment'. In Buddhism, a sadhana is a Mahayana (and in Tibetan Buddhism, typically, Vajrayana) practice where the practitioner recites and meditates on a liturgy invoking the Buddha in a particular form, interacts with that form using the seven branches of prayer and so on and recites the name or the mantra of that form in order to receive the adhistana. The point of a sadhana is that one practices it regularly until it really takes over one's heart and mind.

Complete success or accomplishment in the practice would be to actually meet the Buddhas face to face.

Samsara (Sanskrit, Tib. khor wa), literally 'the turning'. It refers to the endless turning or wandering round and round in an endless succession of lives each characterised by suffering. It is existence as experienced by unenlightened beings, whether it's the tread-mill of living from day to day, going nowhere except into old age and death, or the suffering of being trapped in delusion from one life to the next.

Sangha (Sanskrit, literally 'assembly', Tib. gendun), literally 'longing for virtue'. The community of the followers of the Buddha. In Buddhist countries it is often used to refer to the monk and nun community, but technically in the Mahayana tradition it refers to the community of Awakened Beings who lead others to Awakening. This is what we refer to when we sing about the 'sangha of Awakening'. The Sangha is responsible for transmitting the Dharma from one generation to the next, once the Buddha has disappeared from the world. These days in the West (and this reflects the original Indian meaning of the term) it is used for any body of Buddhist practitioners who develop a sense of spiritual community. This is the sense we use the term when we call ourselves the 'Awakened Heart Sangha'.

Sutra (Sanskrit, Tib. do). Texts claimed to have been spoken by the Buddha, or spoken in his presence and approved by him. Thus they are the principal authoritative source for the teachings within the

Buddhist tradition. There are various collections of sutras, some in Pali (used by Theravadin Buddhists) and some in Sanskrit and Chinese. The Chinese were particularly prone to call important texts within their tradition 'sutras' even though there is no pretence of their having been spoken by the historical Buddha. Questions of historical accuracy do not need to concern us, as the important point from the point of view of the tradition is that the teaching is authentic and carries the adhistana of the Buddha, the Awakened One. The true Sutra is a spiritual revelation of a mandala that exists in some timeless sense forever, and can be entered like a kind of world by any being who has contact with it at any level. Hence sutras are treated as sacred objects, almost like people in many Buddhist traditions.

Upadesha (Sanskrit, Tib. mengak), meaning special oral instruction. Upadesha refers to oral meditation instructions r particularly those associated with linking into the true nature of Reality, that are given live to the student based on the experience and realisation of the teacher. This contrasts with teachings that are given by rote or from texts. The latter kind of transmission involves faithfully preserving the word s as vehicles for the meaning. Upadesha involves finding the right words or even situations to trigger transmission of the meaning. Sometimes upadesha might be couched in terms that are never found in texts and formal teachings, but get at the meaning behind those teachings in a more direct and effective way. Upadesha is therefore interactive and tends to reflect the problems and approach of a particular time and place. Over the centuries collections have been made of upadesha, so that these teachings have become part of the literary tradition. For this reason, somewhat ironically, there are many texts which call themselves upadesha. There is no essential difference between upadesha and 'pointing out instructions' (ngo tro) or 'introductions to the nature of mind' although the latter term usually refers to very significant upadesha that actually brings about realisation in a very immediate and powerful way.

Yogin (Sanskrit, Tib. Naljorpa; female yogini). Someone who practices yoga, but not here referring to a practitioner of the physical exercises associated with hatha yoga! Yoga means to join and comes from the same root as yoke; in the context of the Tibetan tradition it refers to linking into the Awakened Heart, the true nature of Reality. Those practitioners who really dedicate themselves to Awakening and work with their direct experience in meditation to accomplish it are known as yogins. The term is understood to refer to those with significant experience and realisation, although a non-expert would not be able to distinguish between an ordinary practitioner and a yogin with any certainty. Sometimes yogins are not recognised until their death, when they show signs of accomplishment, thus proving that they had been no ordinary practitioners. Often retreatants or people regarded as really good practitioners are referred to as yogins as a sign of respect for what they are doing.

Shenpen Hookham

Shenpen Hookham is the principal teacher of the Awakened Heart Sangha. In the 1970s she spent 6 years as a nun in India, training under Tibetan teachers such as Karma Thinley Rinpoche, Kalu Rinpoche and Bokar Rinpoche. She has spent 9 years in retreat and for the last 20 years has been a close student of Khenpo Tsultrim Gyamtso Rinpoche. Khenpo Rinpoche is one of the foremost living teachers of the Kagyu tradition of Tibetan Buddhism, a great scholar and master of meditation. On his instructions Shenpen completed a doctoral thesis published as 'The Buddha Within'. He is so well satisfied with her understanding and meditation experience, that he has encouraged her, as lama, to teach Mahamudra, the innermost teachings of the Kagyu tradition. For the last 20 year she has taught alongside her husband, Rigdzin Shikpo, who has been a great source of inspiration and guidance for her. Rigdzin Shikpo was a close student of the late Chogyam Trungpa Rinpoche and is a great practitioner of Dzogchen, the innermost teachings of the Nyingma tradition of Tibetan Buddhism.

For further information about the Awakened Heart Sangha, please contact:

Awakened Heart Sangha, Ynys Graianog, Criccieth, Gwynedd, LL52 0NT

Tel: 01766 530839 Email: office@ahs.org.uk Web: www.ahs.org.uk

Printed in Great Britain
by Amazon